DATE DUE

NO~~ ~~		
DEZ 1 02		

PLACES
OF WORSHIP

The Nearby History Series
David E. Kyvig, *Series Editor*
Myron A. Marty, *Consulting Editor*

Nearby History: Exploring the Past Around You
by Kyvig and Marty (1982)

Volume 1
Local Schools
by Ronald E. Butchart (1986)

Volume 2
Houses and Homes
by Barbara J. Howe, Dolores A. Fleming,
Emory L. Kemp, and Ruth Ann Overbeck (1987)

Volume 3
Public Places
by Gerald A. Danzer (1987)

Volume 4
Places of Worship
by James P. Wind (1990)

Places of Worship

Exploring Their History

James P. Wind

American Association for State and Local History
Nashville, Tennessee

To Preslyn and Roberta Wind
for introducing me to congregational life and
awakening early interest in nearby history.

Published by the American Association for State and Local History, an international non-profit membership organization. For membership information, please contact Director of Membership Services, (615) 255-2971.

Library of Congress Cataloging-in-Publication Data

Wind, James P., 1948-
    Places of worship : exploring their history / James P. Wind
        p.   cm. — (The Nearby history series ; v. 4)
    Includes bibliographical references.
    ISBN 0-942063-04-X : $14.95
    1. Parishes—United States—Historiography. 2. United States—Religion—Societies, etc.—
Historiography. 3. United States—History, Local—Historiography. I. Title. II. Series.
BR515.W56   1990   89-39919
291.6'5'0722—dc20   CIP

Contents

Editors' Introduction

INDIVIDUALS, FAMILIES, LOCAL ORGANIZATIONS AND institutions, and communities instinctively know that their own history is important to them. If they can recall nothing of that past, they are in the same position as people suffering from amnesia, unable to remember from where they came, how they responded to needs or challenges, what produced successes or setbacks, from whence they drew affection and support, or opposition, and where they intended to go. History, much like memory, helps identify familiar elements in new situations, provides a guide to appropriate behavior, and offers a standard of comparison across time and circumstance. In this sense, history is far more than a remembrance of things past, though it certainly includes that. History represents a means of coming to terms with the present, developing an awareness of the power of previous influences, the continuities or distinctiveness in current conditions, and the range of future possibilities. Just as memory helps the individual avoid having to repeat the same discoveries, behaviors, and mistakes, historical knowledge helps the individual, group, institution, or community avoid starting from scratch each time an issue needs to be addressed.

The value of historical understanding of the nearby world equals that of national and international history. English historian H.P.R. Finberg considered "the family, the local community, the national state, and the supra-national society as a series of concentric circles." He observed, "Each requires to be studied with constant reference to the one outside it; but the inner rings are not the less perfect circles for being wholly surrounded and enclosed by the outer." Indeed, there is great utility in knowledge of the past of the world close at hand, for it is this history that shapes the circumstances we must deal with directly and constantly.

Even if the value of historical understanding is obvious, the means of acquiring it are usually less evident, especially when the subject of interest is local, previously unexplored, and of concern primarily to a small population. Most of us have acquired most of our knowledge of the past from books, teachers, museums, films, or other presentations. What is one to do if the subject has never been explored, if there is no book on the topic in the library, if there is no expert to whom to turn?

What is to be done in the even more likely circumstance that answers obtained from such sources are insufficient or unsatisfying? The prospect of undertaking original historical research oneself is understandably daunting.

The Nearby History series is based on the premise that history is not only useful, but is also accessible. Any literate person, motivated to explore some question regarding the past of his or her immediate surroundings, can master most appropriate historical techniques, pursue most research possibilities, critically evaluate most potential explanations, and achieve a considerable measure of understanding. In 1982 we wrote a book that argued the importance of taking a look at the history of the close-at-hand world and attempted to assist readers in doing so. We intended *Nearby History: Exploring the Past Around You* as merely a general introduction to a broad and complex topic. The book sought to raise questions for consideration, point out the sorts of materials that exist for historical research, suggest generally how they might be used, and indicate some of the published works on nearby historical topics that might offer useful models or comparisons. *Nearby History* was predicated on the belief that inquiry into the nearby past was not an undertaking for academic professionals alone but could be pursued in a worthwhile fashion by any interested student or out-of-school adult. The warm reception which greeted *Nearby History* encouraged us to carry this notion further by providing specific advice on exploring particular topics. The Nearby History series has thus far considered schools, homes, and public places and now turns its attention to places of worship.

Whether Christian churches, Jewish synagogues, Islamic mosques, Buddhist temples, or the gathering places of other faiths, places of worship are important to their own community of members or supporters, and they are important to the larger communities of which they are a part. Their belief systems, their customs and practices, the people they attract and also that they may repel, and their social, economic, and political practices can have quite an impact outside as well as inside their own walls. These communities are, in fact, among the most complex of all local institutions. Coming to understand the history of a nearby place of worship can be a worthwhile undertaking in its own right, and it is certainly an essential element in coming to terms with the history of the community of which it forms a part.

Places of Worship: Exploring Their History by James P. Wind offers the insights of an experienced and able historian of American religion as to how to investigate the past of any community of faith, regardless of doctrine, denomination, or circumstance. Wind takes as his focus the individual congregation, using this term in the broad sense throughout the book to refer to any group which clusters together due to shared belief or practice, rather than the narrow sense of a particular Christian denomination. This unusual approach has produced a unique research guide, one which should prove highly useful to historians of individual churches. Using vivid illustrations — from traditional and unconventional; eastern, midwestern, and western; rural and urban; wealthy and modest; large and small; as well as Jewish, Catholic, and Protestant congregations — James Wind points out questions which may be asked and suggests ways in which answers may be sought. In two valuable appendices, he calls attention to some of the most helpful published work on individual American religions and provides a directory of denominational archives and historical agencies. Perhaps his greatest contribution is to call attention to the need to consider any religious community as a dynamic, evolving social organism and not merely a fixed physical structure, organization, and body of doctrine.

Places of Worship seeks to encourage and guide those interested in the history of individual communities of faith to explore that past. Whether one is embarking on such an investigation for the first time or is looking for fresh perspectives on a subject of long-standing interest, the reader should find much of value in this volume of the Nearby History series.

DAVID E. KYVIG, Editor
MYRON A. MARTY, Consulting Editor

Illustrations

THE AUTHOR AND PUBLISHER GRATEFULLY ACKNOWLEDGE the following individuals and organizations for granting permission to reproduce, on the pages listed below, pictorial material from their collections.

First United Methodist Church (Evanston, Illinois), pp. 49, 50, 51, 53, 54, 56
Idaho State Historical Society, pp. 70, 71
Micah Marty, pp. 3, 52
National Archives, p. 6
Derek Olson, cover; pp. xiv, xx, 4, 6, 7, 10, 29, 30, 32, 47

Permissions for reprinted material as follows:

Beacon Press, p. 7—from *The Structure of Praise* by Arthur Mazmanian. Copyright 1970 by Beacon Press.

First United Methodist Church (Meridian, Idaho), p. 73—from *They Came to Build a Community* by Lila Hill and Glen W. Davidson. Copyright 1986 by First United Methodist Church, Meridian, Idaho.

Harper & Row, Publishers, Inc., p. 26—from *Small Churches are Beautiful*, edited by Jackson W. Carroll. Copyright 1977 by The Hartford Seminary Foundation.

C. Frank Johnson, p. 72—from *They Came to Build a Community* by Lila Hill and Glen W. Davidson. Copyright 1986 by First United Methodist Church, Meridian, Idaho.

University of Pittsburgh Press, pp. 11, 13—from *Community in a Black Pentecostal Church: An Anthropological Study* by Melvin D. Williams. Copyright 1974 by the University of Pittsburgh Press.

Acknowledgments

MY INTEREST IN PLACES OF WORSHIP HAS SEVERAL sources. As a clergyman, my training and vocational orientation has always been toward "the parish." Years of service in the ministry have only sharpened that original interest.

Graduate training in church history helped me set congregational reality into the larger religious and social contexts which surround it. During those years when I looked at everything but places of worship an agenda of questions was building for a new look at these institutions.

Near the end of my student days at the Divinity School of the University of Chicago, Martin E. Marty, my advisor, and Franklin I. Gamwell, my dean, invited me to direct a research project evaluating congregational studies in America. That invitation brought together my early interest and my more recent studies.

A grant from Lilly Endowment, Inc., made possible two years of inquiry into recent attempts to study American congregations. The Endowment's Senior Vice President, Robert W. Lynn, provided invaluable counsel about those projects and even more important encouragement to complete a daunting assignment. When I began to sense the need for congregational history to make its contribution to this field, more encouragement followed.

As my inquiry into congregational studies proceeded I had opportunity to meet with many of the important contributors to the field. They will easily spot their influence on my thinking in the pages that follow. But here each should be acknowledged: Don S. Browning, Jackson W. Carroll, Jay Dolan, Carl Dudley, Andrew Greeley, Neil Gillman, Robert Gribbon, the late James F. Hopewell, David Leege, Loren Mead, Philip Murnion, C. Ellis Nelson, David A. Roozen, Douglas A. Walrath, Jack Wertheimer, Barbara Wheeler, Melvin Williams.

At another level — a very important one — I wish to acknowledge those who contributed to the shaping of this manuscript. Editors David E. Kyvig and Myron A. Marty have been as patient, encouraging, and helpful as any author could hope for. Lucille Ott and Marion Miller made efficient work of all the corrections and changes incorporated into the second draft. Dorothy Bass, DeAne Lagerquist, James W. Lewis, and

xi

Martin E. Marty made helpful suggestions as critical readers. The two appendices to this volume would not exist without the painstaking work of research assistants, Jennifer Browne and Michael Dodge. Derek Olson and Micah Marty provided invaluable assistance with photographs and illustrations.

Finally, my family has kept this project and its author moving towards completion with humor and grace. To Joshua and Rachel, the answer to their "what are you working on" question is — and not a moment too soon! — no longer "the congregation book." Kathleen's contribution as listener, questioner, and nudger is larger than she knows. Sharing a family pew with them has been one of the primary resources for this book.

Preface

THEY SEEM TO TURN UP ALMOST EVERYWHERE. THEY come in an unending variety of shapes, sizes, styles, and colors. Some are older than our nation, others will come to life long after this book has been read, used, and forgotten. Some dominate their horizons, others blend into their environments so well that only the insider or the skilled observer can find them. They are sources of meaning and hope for more Americans than any other single type of voluntary organization. They also can disappoint, alienate, confuse, and bore people in ways that few other institutions can.

The *they* in the preceding paragraph refers to places of worship — congregations, churches, parishes, synagogues, mosques, ashrams, temples and other forms of enduring religious communities that have found their places on the American landscape. As the pictures on the facing page suggest, the diversity and pluriformity of these religious institutions defy glib generalizations. There are so many of them that we cannot count them, despite heroic efforts of statisticians at places like the National Council of Churches. Their *1989 Yearbook*, for example, reports these figures for 1988: 143,830,806 Americans belong to 349,381 congregations in the 219 denominations that send them statistical summaries. And those figures, sizeable as they are, miss countless unaffiliated churches, or the congregations that have escaped the statistician's eye due to poor or non-existent records.

Moreover, these American statistics are only a fraction of the whole! While this book will focus on North America, it is important to note, if only in passing, the much wider context. A fascinating table in the 1982 edition of *World Christian Encyclopedia* provides some clues. In 1970, statisticians counted 1,506,360 Christian congregations around the world. 1,131,809,580 of the world's inhabitants were affiliated with these institutions, which were scattered across 18,162 denominations. A brief decade later, these experts counted 1,718,404 Christian congregations, with 1,323,386,867 members, in 20,781 denominations. Clearly the worldwide congregational story is much larger and grows much more rapidly than most of us imagine.

Meganumbers like these do not tell the whole story, but they do tell

Clockwise from upper left: St. Nicholas Ukrainian Catholic Cathedral; New Light Missionary Baptist Church; Islamic Cultural Center of Greater Chicago; Illinois Institute of Technology Chapel. (All in the greater Chicago area.)

us part of one. Jewish, Islamic, Buddhist and other non-Christian groups do not show up in these figures, but they and a host of religionists old and new are out there, congregating, participating in one of the most important and most overlooked forms of human behavior.

Equally as amazing as the proliferation of these religious entities throughout the world and in this so-called secular land, is how unnoticed these institutions remain. It is hard to miss a cathedral like St. Paul's which dominates the skyline of St. Paul, Minnesota, or the modern lines of Eliel Saarinen's Tabernacle Church of Christ in Columbus, Indiana, or the Crystal Cathedral of Robert Schuller in Garden Grove, California. Yet while such prominent buildings catch the eye of the expressway driver, we tend to be no more aware of most places of worship than we are of filling stations or drugstores. In the course of the day we pass many, but pay attention to them only when there is specific reason for stopping in. Like most automobile drivers who selectively screen from their consciousness all but one or two types of stations which feature certain brands of gasoline, most moderns, if they pay attention at all to the congregations in their vicinity, will tend to be aware of only a few of the many varieties around them.

Sadly, this fleeting and selective awareness is not only characteristic of the casual passerby. Civic and religious leaders, social and religious historians, and even most congregation members themselves seem equally unaware. When challenged many of these people will acknowledge that these institutions are important. Yet in the pursuit of their everyday responsibilities they, like the public in general, tend to take the churches, synagogues, and parishes of the land for granted. A host of assumptions about the irrelevance of these institutions to most of modern life, about the relationship of public to private life, and about the basic sameness of congregations in spite of all their obvious social, denominational, ethnic and political diversity, serves to buttress a prevailing mindset which skips over the most basic religious institution of our age.

This book on exploring the history of places of worship seeks to provide resources for those who *have* noticed congregations and who now wish to delve more deeply into the past of individual parishes, synagogues, and churches. It offers angles of vision on the rich thicket of reality present in almost every one of these religious institutions. Each chapter attempts to help both first time and seasoned historians find new questions and approaches which can open up forgotten or ignored aspects of congregational life to those living within these religious communities or near them. The book begins with consideration of several distinct ways of looking at these institutions. Its middle section first examines the tools and raw materials a historian uses to build a narrative and then offers suggestions about writing the final product. A concluding chapter suggests a much larger significance for congregational history writing than we are accustomed to — its more ambitious rationale should encourage historians to take this kind of inquiry very seriously. It may also help congregations glimpse more of their own importance than previously noticed.

Different people read books like this one in different ways. Most will read from front to back, occasionally inserting a thumb to glance ahead or check back to something referred to earlier. That approach allows this book's logic to make its step-by-step progression. Others will read individual chapters as specific questions arise. For example, some may begin with chapters on the historian's questions and building blocks, and then turn to chapters on first impressions and landscapes. Both approaches have merits. To those in a hurry to get to work in the archives of a place of worship the second approach will have considerable appeal. Those who wish to begin by identifying a congregation's "feeling tone" will gravitate towards the first. Neither approach is necessarily better, as long as readers remember that this book intends to explore a variety of essential dimensions in the life of any place of worship.

In order to keep a focus on the common enterprise of history writing which is to be pursued in such a rich variety of settings as America offers, I have chosen the phrase "congregational history" to describe the task which confronts readers of this book. The adjective "congregational" can be misleading. To many "congregational" will suggest a type of polity, or church organization associated with denominations which trace their origins to Puritan England. Roman Catholics, however, use "congregation" to describe departments or divisions in the Vatican hierarchy, such as their Sacred Congregation for the Doctrine of the Faith. Traditionally, they have used "parish" to describe what Protestants refer to as "congregation."

Neither the Protestant nor the Catholic use is intended here. Instead, the term seeks to capture an important type of human behavior which takes place across denominational lines, in synagogues, parishes, churches as well as other congregations. The *Oxford English Dictionary* provides support for such a use of *congregation* with this broad definition: "A body of people assembled for religious worship or to hear a preacher. (The most common use.)" The *OED* fills in the idea with a subsequent definition: "The body of persons who habitually attend or belong to a particular place of worship." In this book, *congregational* will refer to these three elements that the *OED* helps identify. A congregation is made up of (1) "a body of people" who (2) "assemble for religious worship" — with or without a preacher! — and (3) "habitually attend-(ing) or belong(ing) to a particular place." People who regularly gather to worship at a particular place are the subjects of the history writing that this book seeks to support.

While historians usually tend to be quite circumspect about stating their assumptions and governing hypotheses, it is important that this book for historians be clear about several assumptions which inform the approach taken here. As this book will make clear, I believe that the study of congregational history can make a significant contribution to both congregational life and to our larger understandings of who we are as people and why we do what we do. Congregational history is not the only important subject in the world, but it is one subject which has its own intrinsic worth and which has been neglected for far too long. Several chapters attest to the importance I attach to working with a variety of perspectives. Insights from anthropologists, sociologists, experts in practical theology and organizational development, urban observers, journalists and historians are essential if we are to understand institutions which are far more complex and far more interesting than most assume.

In addition, if it is to be done well, congregational history must be a communal enterprise. Its very subject matter, the life of communities of faith, suggests this communal character. And history, that noble discipline which seeks to be an all-encompassing field, is particularly well suited to a study of communities from a variety of perspectives. It is the strength of the historical approach to welcome the insights and discoveries gleaned from many vantage points. Thus on many occasions this book will draw upon the wisdom of others and encourage historians to consult with a variety of people. Although a written history is usually the work of one hand, that hand should not belong to a lone ranger who rides into and out of a congregation's story in solitude. Rather, the hand should be that of someone who has been a lively conversation partner with many — both living and dead. And, quite often, the final product will be the result of a very lively collaboration which produced a better book than one prepared single-handedly.

Another assumption is that the experience of strangers can illumine our own. Unlike many denominational resources for congregational historians, this book deliberately seeks to take historians on detours through a variety of congregational worlds which may seem quite unfamiliar. The individual seeking to make sense of a half century of life in her mid-sized Baptist church in an Atlanta suburb may be tempted to skip over discussions of a Reform Jewish synagogue in Boston, an inner city black Pentecostal church in Pittsburgh or a rural congregation in Idaho. But if fresh ways of opening up the yellowed pages of her church's board of trustees minutes or reading between the lines of its founding pastor's now quite dated sermons are sought, such detours become important parts of the historian's journey.

One more assumption merits mention. In the midst of all the names, dates, and places which so delight historians are central concerns about who humans are, how they change and stay the same over various periods of time, and how they understand what happens to them. Congregations are remarkable laboratories for isolating key changes in human thinking and acting. Their traditions often mask innovations while their dramatic shifts in practice and belief are frequently preceded and followed by many smaller and more subtle transitions which bear elements of the past — both distant and recent — within them. To embark on a venture into congregational history is to set out to answer questions that have preoccupied humans in all of their endeavors.

A final assumption seems obvious but easily could be lost sight of once the fascinating details and lines of inquiry pursued by historians come into view. Congregations *are* places of worship. They are the special places in our culture where people relate to the holy, search for the sacred, address God. While congregation members do many other things, they also worship a transcendent source of life. Many of the elements of congregational history can be found in other zones of life — economic, political, social, psychological. Even the quest for the holy occasionally leads beyond these official places of worship. Yet these institutions are distinctive because — like in no other — humans regularly come together within them for the purpose of expressing ultimate concerns and meanings. Thus historians who consider congregations have the special challenge of relating this distinctive and constitutive part of their identities to a myriad of everyday activities and behaviors. This book cannot do justice to the variety of ways congregations express sacredness. But it can remind each historian of this fundamental dimension and urge them to bring their particular congregation's religious character to the center of their inquiry. Each of the questions and perspectives attended to in the pages that follow has the potential — no matter how secular looking — of revealing an aspect of this religious dimension of congregational identity.

The primary goals of this book are: 1. that the study of this fundamental but overlooked zone of human life might contribute to ongoing attempts to understand who we are, where we come from, why we do what we do, and where we are going; and 2. that such understanding might enrich the institutions where some of people's deepest aspirations and most profound questions are expressed. The relationship of these universal human concerns to the particularities of one local place of worship is what makes congregational history so interesting. Finding ways to open up the ordinary-looking life of a congregation so that its extraordinary richness may be seen is the challenge before us.

For Further Reading

Those interested in national and global congregational trends should consult Constant H. Jacquet, editor, *Yearbook of American and Canadian Churches, 1989* (Nashville: Abingdon Press, 1989), and David B. Barrett, editor, *The World Christian Encyclopedia* (Oxford: Oxford University Press, 1982).

Baha'i House of Worship, Evanston, Illinois.

PLACES
OF WORSHIP

·1·

First Impressions

"EARLY IMPRESSIONS ARE HARD TO ERADICATE FROM THE mind. When once wool has been dyed purple, who can restore it to its previous whiteness?" These ancient words from St. Jerome, the fifth-century church father, carry an appropriate warning for modern congregational historians. Occasionally a church, synagogue, or parish history will be written by an individual who has the advantage — and, from many angles, disadvantage — of a fresh encounter with a congregation. For such a historian, everything about that particular congregation will be new.

The historian who approaches a congregation as an outsider has the difficult job of sifting and weighing "early impressions" in order to form a portrait which bears more than a superficial likeness to its subject. It is easy to let the attention-getting sounds heard in first encounters drown out other more subtle motifs in a congregation's repertoire of experiences. The disenchantment of a former parish leader, or the effervescence of a new minister can skew a portrait, staining first impressions an idiosyncratic gray or rose color which may have been only a short seasonal coloration in the congregation's longer life.

Jerome's caveat is equally apt for longtime congregation members who become insider-historians. Familiarity may not always breed contempt, but it almost inevitably fosters selective vision. Just as a grandparent may sit in a favored reading chair day after day, year after year, and never seem bothered by its worn arms or discolored fabric, so a congregation member can become quite comfortable with the furnishings of a particular congregational habitat. The out-of-tune organ, the tattered hymnals, the hopelessly antiquated bookkeeping system, the faded

1

portrait of a cherished religious figure, don't seem bothersome because this place feels like home.

At other times, however, familiarity does breed contempt and attention can be so riveted to "that" bothersome organ, hymnal, accounting system, or portrait that nothing else — even the remarkable and praiseworthy — in a congregation's life seems capable of gaining notice. In both cases, early impressions become lasting mindsets, habits of thinking about congregations that focus upon certain aspects to the exclusion of others. The member functions like an absentminded photographer who forgets about the filter left on the camera and cannot figure out why every picture taken — no matter what time of day or year, speed of film, or angle taken on the subject — comes out the same color. Insider historians can — unless they become aware of their early impressions — end up missing out on much that is colorful and important in the congregational story they tell.

The purpose of this chapter is to help early impressions work for rather than against the congregational historian. By taking detours first into the stately world of medieval cathedrals, then into the more immediate context of a modern black church, and finally into the fresh vistas opened by a new method for studying congregations, readers can become more sensitive to the power of early impressions in shaping the subsequent histories they may write. On the one hand, it is important for longtime church members to learn how to reperceive their congregations — to see them as if for the first time and to notice all of the elements which usually go overlooked. On the other, outsider historians and those who can temporarily suspend their "insiderhood" and become at least partial outsiders, need to seize the opportunity afforded by early impressions. There is much that can be learned about a congregation before familiarity settles in.

Little details that get lost after "strangeness" wears off — where people sit during worship, what they wear, how they treat newcomers — are often important clues to a congregation's character and history. By carefully gathering first impressions, congregational historians can often open up lines of inquiry which will make their narratives more insightful and much more complete. When armed with a bit of suspicion about what will be found in these early approaches, the congregational historian can set a sizable agenda for further work by simply looking around and paying attention to all that is there.

From the Outside In: An Architectural Detour

A good way to begin is to work from the outside in. Each of the detours taken in this chapter moves us deeper into a congregation's present life — revealing many of its facets and dimensions. So, pause for a moment on the opposite side of the street and take a long and careful look at the building that houses "your" particular congregation. What does that building say about this group of people? To help sharpen that question accompany me on detour number one — into the rich history of ecclesiastical architecture. By taking a look at several examples of medieval places of worship, the congregational historian can find new ways to look at the particular building that will be the source of many early impressions.

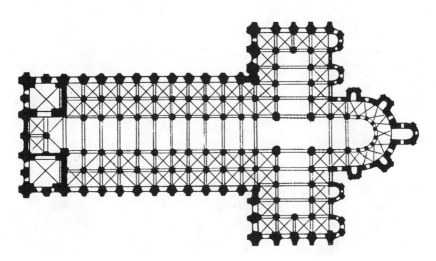

Cruciform floorplan of Gothic Cathedral. Black dots represent stone pillars; thin lines indicate vaulted ceiling.

No single building type could make this point more immediately or more forcefully than the medieval cathedral of Europe. Few readers of this book will write about these great symbols of the religious and social life of earlier generations. Yet each can gain fresh perspective from an encounter with their soaring arches, leaded glass, carved stone, and graceful spires. Built in days when literacy was the prerogative of elites, cathedrals were textbooks of faith for the common people. In silent but powerful ways they told the story of the Christian faith. The dominant shape of the cross — expressed in the language of floorplan and stone carving — bore witness to Christianity's central image. Baptistry and altar gave spatial prominence to the two great sacraments which were indispensible points of contact between believers and their God. The multitude of saints who took their places in niches over doorways and in windows reminded new generations of Christians that many had lived and died in this faith and that one day those ranks would include another generation — their own. One could absorb the central elements of the faith from the walls and artworks of these buildings — they preached, encouraged, reminded, and pointed ahead.

Icon of Virgin and Child, St. Joseph's Ukrainian Catholic Church, Chicago, Illinois.

The cathedrals also revealed how people in the twelfth and thirteenth centuries thought about God. Stern statues of Christ as judge, warmer ones of Mary as mother, paintings of the Creation and the End Times all revealed not only ideas and events from earlier centuries but the way artists, patrons, parishes, or communities understood the relationships between God and humanity. These revelatory buildings disclosed not only the central elements of the great tradition of the Christian faith but also many nuances of local custom and culture.

One of the pre-eminent students of this type of architecture,

Otto von Simson, claims that the "Gothic cathedral originated in the religious experience, the metaphysical speculation, in the political and even the physical realities, of twelfth-century France, and the genius of those who created it." His reasearch led him to conclude that there was a "singular nexus of living forces" in the Gothic form, a form to which subsequent generations have become "curiously blind." It is that intermingling of religion, philosophy, politics, and physical reality which escapes notice of so many cathedral and congregation visitors — and which is so crucial to congregational historians. The "early impressions" problem plagues even those who step for the first time into as great a cathedral as Chartres. Or as von Simson put it, "The vision that originally challenged the material resources, the technical ingenuity, the consummate artistry of an entire age, has long since become a commonplace of respectable church building and an object of archaeological classification."

Gothic cathedrals from the middle ages are not the subject of this book and von Simson's analysis is much too complex to be recounted here. But his conclusion about the Abbey of St. Denis, the prototype of the Gothic cathedral, should at least raise new questions for congregational historians. This "new" (1144 C.E.) cathedral was designed by the Abbot Suger, a long forgotten clergyman who played in his day a role similar to Cardinal Richelieu in the eighteenth century or Henry Kissinger in our own. This abbot was the key political advisor to King Louis VI and leader of the most powerful religious institution in twelfth-century France. Suger intended for his new church building to be, like other cathedrals of Europe "an image of heaven." But embroidered around that theological image was a blueprint for a Christian France which featured the Abbey of St. Denis as its religious capitol and its abbot as the religious primate of the nation. In other words, one can look at this building and find traces of a "grand design" which included not only a religious community, but an entire nation. "Suger undertook the rebuilding of his church in order to implement his master plan in the sphere of politics. His vision as a statesman imposed itself upon the architectural project; he conceived it as the monumental expression of that vision. Not only as a shrine but as a work of art the sanctuary was to eclipse the great pilgrimage centers of western Europe; it was to bear comparison . . . with Constantinople and in a sense with Jerusalem."

Most of the congregations in our modern religious environment have

Clockwise from upper left: K.A.M. - Temple Isaiah Israel, Chicago, Illinois; St. Paul's Norwegian Lutheran Church, Irwin, Iowa; St. Joseph's Ukrainian Catholic Church, Chicago, Illinois; St. Paul's Cathedral, St. Paul, Minnesota.

Differing expressions of holiness (clockwise from upper left): Simple colonial pulpit of Rocky Hill Meeting House, Amesbury, Massachusetts; Ark for Torah, K.A.M. - Temple Isaiah Israel, Chicago, Illinois; Altar of Midwest Buddhist Temple, Chicago, Illinois; Altar of St. Joseph's Ukrainian Catholic Church, Chicago, Illinois.

not been products of the grand designs or visions that fired the imagination of people like Abbot Suger. More modest purposes will usually be found. But this detour to twelfth-century France should serve as a stimulus to prod congregational historians to search for the concealed "nexus" of factors which converged to give rise to the particular building which serves as home for a congregation. What vision served as foundation for this particular structure? What motives were present in the minds of the planners? What stories can be told if one learns to read the building's architectural and aesthetic grammar?

Skill in interpreting the nuances of architectural languages takes years of study and building watching to acquire. Most congregational historians need not master this specialized field. Instead they can develop sensitivity to one important source of information about a congregation. When the stones refuse to speak, or when the building's message remains unintelligible, the historian can turn to a number of resources for help. Perhaps there is a professional architect in the congregation or neighborhood. If not, public and university libraries have shelves of resources which may be useful. And there are specialized books on church architecture — some quite scholarly like von Simson's and others aimed at a wider audience — which are worth an hour or two of browsing and spot reading.

One way to increase ability in reading a church building is to consider initial samples of church and synagogue architecture provided in the accompanying photographs. These offer only a first glance of the rich variety of grammars and syntaxes provided by American congregations. Yet a few moments spent poring over these examples can suggest even to a first time observer the distinctive features and idioms of church buildings. The types of structures presented here and elsewhere in this book provide an architectural spectrum within which a historian can situate a particular building.

It is not enough to look at the outside of these buildings for clues about a congregation's architectural diction; the interiors also have much to say. As these pictures show, the way furniture is arranged, the focal points of vision, the types of artwork employed all testify to sensibilities that carry theological understandings, cultural assumptions, social aspirations and aesthetic canons. Because history is concerned with how things change over time, the careful observer will also want to look for signs of architectural change within buildings, those subtle indicators of new perspectives, needs, and theological understandings which may have entered a congregation in the years following building construction. Evidence for changing understandings of the relationship between God and humans can be found in the rearrangements of a chancel. When altars move closer to people, or clergy and worshippers pull down some of their architectural barriers, something is happening to basic beliefs about divine–human interaction. Sometimes congregations outgrow their buildings — frequently more than once. Occasionally they move into somebody else's sacred space. Shifts in style from one building to the next can also be important clues of subtle changes in congregational membership, attitudes, and self images.

Watching People

Bricks and mortar, as fascinating as they can be when shaped by varying religious communities, are only a part of a congregational story. Although many historians may be tempted to linger over this or that fascinating detail of a particular building, they dare not confuse a building with the flesh and blood of a congregation, its people. At best, buildings provide clues about a congregation at certain key moments in its life — the time of its founding, or the time of a move to a new location, or the time when sufficient dis-ease about an old architectural or artistic style existed to motivate a congregation to rearrange the furniture or redesign its home. Changes in a building may provide clues to the ways in which a congregation participated in a larger plot (something which will be discussed in chapter 6). Was the relocated altar a sign of involvement in a movement of liturgical renewal? Does the new building reflect a major shift in American architecture? Answers to such questions can link congregations to significant stories beyond their own.

Church buildings also allude to implicit congregational styles which may or may not be in effect at the time the historian enters the scene. The Italians who built a central city Romanesque cathedral may have moved to the suburbs, replaced by Hispanic immigrants who now occupy the same building but express their faith in very different ways. Black Baptists may find a nineteenth-century Jewish temple congenial to their twentieth-century purposes. Thus architectural clues need to be unearthed, followed up, and put into context. Most importantly, they

In 1922 Pilgrim Baptist Church moved into this building designed by Dankmar Adler and Louis Sullivan when Kehilath Anshe Ma'ariv Synagogue moved to a new Chicago community.

must be surrounded by the human texture of the congregation's members.

How does a historian let the people of the congregation become a part of the story? One way is to ransack the archives, diaries, file drawers, and memories of congregation members for traces of the people who gave life to their congregation. That important phase of history writing is the subject of a later chapter. Another way, one that has only recently been developed and has yet to be discovered by congregational historians, is for the historian to become what anthropologists call a "participant-observer." Whether entering a church or synagogue for the first time or the five hundredth, a congregational historian can assume a stance which will allow previously overlooked aspects of a religious community's life to come into view. Rather than discuss a formal definition of the participant-observer, I intend to take the reader on the second detour of

Formal Organization of Zion Church.

KEY:
Vertical position indicates relative status.
―――― indicates line of influence.

this chapter — one that follows a skilled ethnographer (participant-observer) into a congregation. The value of the detour is that it presents several new questions about congregational life.

Zion Holiness Church is a pseudonym for a black Pentecostal congregation in Pittsburgh. Melvin D. Williams spent a fruitful year in this place of worship as a participant-observer, learning about its inner workings. He attended its events, ate its dinners, and joined in its worship. By systematically stopping to think about what he experienced, Williams opened up Zion's life in a way that provides insights into overlooked dimensions of congregational life. His agenda was different from that of most congregational historians. As a professional anthropologist, Williams' approach was "not primarily designed to analyze and describe the religious characteristics" of Zion. Instead, he wanted to study "the distinctive quality of social relations, communal ideology, and social behavior within the group," which are closely related to religion, but not its essence. He gave little attention to the historical side of Zion's story, restricting his attention to powerful immediate impressions.

The people who belonged to Zion were primarily uprooted black southerners who had participated in an extensive northward migration that began in 1915 and still continues. These people tended to be poor and largely marginal to mainstream American culture. Inside Zion, however, they created a subculture which allowed them to perpetuate many of the values of the rural southern way of life they had left behind. Furthermore, Zion also provided an alternative status system for a group with little likelihood of achieving anything but minimal success in the dominant culture. While their nonchurch world may have been filled with familial and community breakdown, Zion provided an alternative "primary group intimacy" — a precious commodity in an urban environment that seemed primarily hostile and alien. Participation in the life of Zion allowed its members to create a "new society" which was a "huddling place for a wide range of 'poor' ghetto Blacks."

How did Williams draw these conclusions? From observations gained in worship services, at dinners, plays, trips and picnics he began to chart the organizational patterns of the congregation's life. He witnessed Zion's grief at funerals and tagged along on moving days when the whole congregation turned out to help a member. In addition he scrutinized the ninety-one official church members, tracking their origins, recording

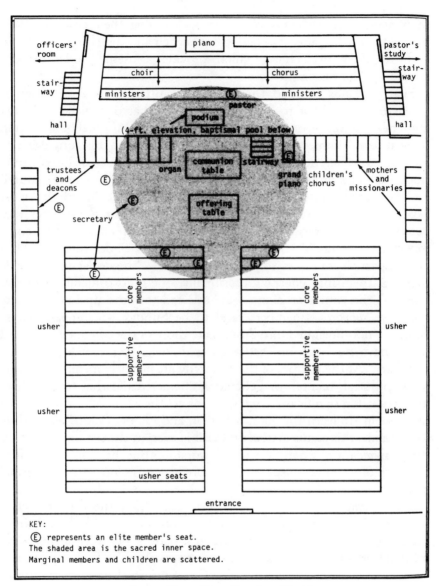

Seating Chart of Zion Church at Worship.

their ages, noting their incomes and observing their congregational behavior. Finally, after his period as participant-observer came to an end, he drew two charts which provide a useful model for the congregational historian.

First Williams mapped the formal organization of Zion Holiness Church. He found it to be quite similar to that of Southern Baptist churches. But his second map which traced Zion's informal organization pattern reveals more about the distinctive features of this congregation. Here status differences became apparent. On the basis of his observations, Williams proposed a typology, or classification system for church members. *Elite* members "raise the most money, demand the most exposure to other church members, plan the church activities and determine church procedure." Beneath them on the status ladder come *core* members who "do not make the plans, but . . . do the work. They do not participate in decision-making, but once the decisions are made they put them into effect." Occasionally, one or two members of this group — the largest at Zion — are selected to move up into the elite category. *Supportive* members tend to be Sunday worshippers whose "lives are not integrated into Zion as are those of the core members, and [who] have no hope of participating in its power structure as elite members." At the bottom of the hierarchy are *marginal* members, people with "physical, mental, or behavioral characteristics that render them ineffectual for significant contributions to the church." These people never seem "to learn the cues, behavior, and idiom of Zion." According to Williams, this status system was visible even in the seating pattern of the congregation when it was at worship. But he also could find evidence of it in every aspect of the congregation's formal and informal life.

In a moment I will raise some cautions about the use of such a typology. But first it is important to learn one or two more lessons from Professor Williams. Regarding the distinction between formal and informal organizational patterns, he suggests that the formal pattern is obvious to almost everyone at Zion. The informal one, on the other hand, tends to be "recognized by some, participated in by most, and manipulated by a few." If he is correct when he claims that it is the informal pattern of organization which is distinctive, then this illusive and perhaps disguised pattern is of special interest to congregational historians. To focus only on the elected leaders or the official organizations of the congregation may result in a congregational history that bears a wearying resemblance to others which share similar denominational, ethnic, or social characteristics. By probing for informal networks and patterns, the historian may stumble on an important clue or two which can help the particular character of a congregation come into view.

The second lesson to take from Williams is his painstaking attention to behavioral signals. On the basis of information gathered by watching what congregation members do and by listening in on a wide variety of congregational conversations — ranging from the formal language of worship to the informal gossip of choir members — Williams discerned a distinctive congregational language and set of symbols which drew elements from several sources. The members of this congregation wove together strands from their rural past, their urban present, and their biblical heritage to create a distinctive way of speaking which served to draw a boundary between their congregation and the rest of the world. Zion's behavior will certainly not be replicated in every American congregation. Yet exposure to Williams' analysis can help a historian develop ears and eyes for what is distinctive.

Not everyone will be comfortable with an approach to a congregation that is as political as Williams'. That discomfort has some merit to it. Status is not the whole story in a congregation's life, even though few churches or synagogues can be found where it is not an important dynamic. Further, people do not always fit as neatly into "types" or categories as Williams would have us believe. In many congregations, people will sit near the pulpit because they want to hear better, or because that is where their parents sat, or because that seat is close to the exit nearest the parking lot. Thus it can be risky to impose Williams' seating chart upon other congregations. A better approach is to ask "What are the distinctive patterns of interaction in this congregation? Which groups exist? How do they function? How is power and status distributed here?" While one may never again be able to attend a church supper without thinking of the status seeking going on there, it is hazardous to reduce complex human behavior like that found in congregations to one explanation — even one as potent as politics.

At the same time it is important to resist the temptation to skip over dimensions of congregational life which reveal motivations that seem too worldly, or non-religious. One of the leading theologians of our era,

James M. Gustafson, tried to help people avoid that mistake when he wrote a book in 1961 called *Treasure in Earthen Vessels*. Gustafson's use of St. Paul's metaphor (II Corinthians 4:7) makes the point that congregations are human communities which bear a precious resource inside them. To leave out their humanness is to oversimplify the portrait being drawn. Gustafson's argument, although developed with a Christian audience in mind, can be useful even for historians seeking to understand non-Christian congregations. By substituting *Judaism* or *Islam* for *Christian* and *synagogue* or *mosque* for "church" in the following quotation, they can join Christian readers in taking a stance towards congregations which will allow their full reality to be grasped. Like Gustafson they can assume

> . . . that there is continuity between the Christian community and other human communities. Common-sense observation makes this indisputable: people gather in appropriate buildings; churches have social hierarchies and political arrangements for the conduct of their affairs; an identifiable historical continuity exists through many generations and centuries; Christians have a common object of loyalty that binds them together. In these respects and others, similarities exist between the Christian community and the state, the nation, voluntary associations for charitable purposes, and many other groups and movements. There may be an irreducible uniqueness, a differentium that distinguishes the Church from all other historical communities, but this does not make it absolutely different in kind. It is subject to the same social and historical processes as other communities, and thus to the same types of investigation. Many of the concepts that illumine the nature of secular communities also illumine the Church.

The historian will want to attend to both the continuities shared by congregations and other human groups on the one hand, and what Gustafson calls "irreducible uniqueness" on the other. In addition, he will pursue these questions throughout a congregation's life, not merely in its most recent experience. Otherwise first impressions can mislead.

Identifying a Congregation's Character

The goal of this chapter has been to sensitize readers to the power and usefulness of these impressions. By taking detours into gothic cathedrals and a black Pentecostal church, I sought to increase or awaken a receptivity to ranges of impressions which can help historians identify a congregation's *genius* — that elusive human element which the *Oxford English Dictionary* defines with phrases like "characteristic disposition," "prevelant feeling," or "distinctive character." Attention to the details of a synagogue building or the patterns of interaction within a parish will help the historian step closer to this genius. But by themselves, the architectural and the anthropological approaches will fail to capture it. To get still closer to the slippery character of a congregation yet another angle of vision is needed.

The third detour of this chapter follows a route taken by the late James F. Hopewell, an Emory University professor who played a leading role in reviving interest in congregational studies during the late 1970s and early 1980s. Hopewell's goal was to study congregations in such a way as to find each one's distinctive *story*. For him the key categories to be used in efforts to understand congregational behavior were plot, setting, and characterization. Like Williams he developed a typology which can help historians ask new questions about their congregations. In his hands, every congregation became a text capable of being interpreted if one approached it correctly.

Hopewell sought to help congregations discover their own identities. By *identity* he meant "the persistent set of beliefs, values, patterns, symbols, stories, and style that makes a congregation distinctive." Employing a stance similar to that of Williams, Hopewell entered congregations as a participant-observer in search of a different goal. He wanted to know how each congregation perceived itself, how it defined "both what it finds itself to be and what it determines to become." Discovery of a congregation's identity involves an identification of the "web of meaning" which integrates or holds it together in its past and present circumstances. The importance of Hopewell's concerns for identity and self-perception cannot be overstated. Historians who rush to the archives or the typewriter without stopping to ask "who are these people?" and "how do they understand themselves?" may fail to penetrate to the marrow of their subject.

To uncover a congregation's identity, Hopewell listened for a *plot* in congregational conversations. He wanted to hear about "historic" events and experiences which left an enduring mark. In keeping with his treatment of congregations as texts, he expected that their plots would *link* with others (in families, denominations, communities, etc.), that they would *thicken* in complex ways, that they would *unfold* as event followed upon event, and that they would *twist* in surprising ways. By asking people to tell their personal stories and to recount the history of their congregation, Hopewell hoped to find a pattern of recurring images, heroes, villains, crises, and turning points which could be fashioned into an overarching congregational plot.

As people told these stories Hopewell also expected that a congregation's "heritage" would come into view. A heritage was "a congregation's acknowledgement of the inheritance of beliefs and practices about the Christian faith and life and the purpose of the church that it has by virtue of being a Christian church and standing in that particular historical stream." Hopewell was writing for a Christian audience, but his point about heritage is also important for those of other faiths. All congregations, even those that boast of being nontraditional, stand within traditions, whether acknowledged or not. Attention to heritage makes it possible for the role of these traditions to be recognized.

Synagogues stand within the great tradition of Judaism, while most American churches are shaped by the great tradition of Christianity. These "great" religious traditions provide a distinctive element which distinguishes congregations from other voluntary groups like the Rotary Club or the League of Women Voters (although one may find vestiges of great traditions in many of these!). Each of these master traditions have in turn proliferated into countless smaller versions as the steadily increasing number of denominations reminds us. Thus to understand a Lutheran congregation in the U.S. one must know something about the magisterial Christian tradition, the Lutheran stream within that great tradition, and then one or more of the denominational tributaries which have branched off from that stream. These provide the initial matrix out of which a congregation's particular story emerges.

But, Hopewell cautions, each congregation has "little" or local traditions which shape great traditions into particular heritages. Only by listening and observing can the "peculiar interpretation" of a Christian tradition, the "operational theology" of a congregation, come into view.

Here emphasis must be placed on the sermons preached, the rituals performed, the symbols used, and the metaphors turned to in the congregation's life. By paying attention to the great and little aspects of a congregation's heritage as they interact in the congregation's plot, Hopewell sought to arrive at a congregation's "fundamental vision," its distinctive and identity-giving way of looking at the world.

Hopewell's strategy for identifying such fundamental visions centers around discovery of a congregation's worldview, the distinctive imaginative setting in which it lives. In addition to the realities of neighborhood, income, educational and ethnic background which make up a congregational context (and which receive more detailed attention below), Hopewell wanted to pay attention to the imaginative dwelling places or thought worlds of congregation members. The perspectives people bring to their environments shape what they see; they make a world that is then lived in as if it were real.

When he looked at congregations Hopewell believed that he could find shared worldviews which bound members together. Further, he felt those worldviews fit the categories of a typology developed by Northrop Frye, a distinguished literary scholar. Some congregations, thus, have *comic* orientations to the world. These congregations are "basically concerned with the development of harmony." *Comic* does not necessarily mean humorous, but it does imply that beneath the complications of life is the possibility of "ultimate peace" or a happy outcome. People who assume comic postures in the world are usually possessors of some "hidden" insight, or *gnostic* secret. A comic congregation, then, would be in possession of some special insight which allows its members to assume an optimistic stance towards life.

Another worldview option for congregations is the *romantic* one. People with this kind of outlook on the world are seekers in pursuit of a great reward. In romantic types of stories, heroes appear who can overcome great obstacles and secure "uncommon blessings." The distinctive feature of this type of stance towards the world is its *charismatic* expectation. *Charismatic* in this case means something more than is usually conveyed in discussions about the Spirit-centered revival movement in mainline churches during the sixties and seventies. Miracles, visions, direct encounters with supernatural powers, and divine interventions into the normal patterns of life are manifestations of a world where extra-human realities intrude into mundane circumstances.

Romantic congregations share an optimistic stance toward the world with comic ones. What sets romantic places of worship apart is their emphasis upon superhuman intrusion rather than secret insight.

The third type of worldview in Hopewell's model is the *tragic*. Like romantic sagas, tragic dramas have heroes and heroines. Tragedies, however, follow their protaganists into decline, defeat, and death at the hands of superior powers. The tone of tragedies is more often that of obedient resignation than thrilling adventure. One lives in a tragic context by submission to decrees from God, laws of nature, or the dealings of fate. A *canonic* style, that is, a respectful adherence to a tested and authoritative way of life with its own special repositories or canons of wisdom, is the appropriate response. For Hopewell tragic congregations are those which expect neither triumph over their immediate circumstances nor secret insight to change things. Instead they find meaning in faithful obedience to a way of life, code of behavior, or set of laws which has been handed down from God.

Hopewell's final category is the *ironic* congregation. Within this perspective one expects no heroes or heroines to deliver anybody from what is in essence a closed universe. *Empirical* clarity about life is what counts. Congregations that fit into this category tend to place their emphasis on understanding how life actually works. They place a premium on the "integrity of simple human experience" and see love between humans as a chief source for hope and meaning. Ironic congregations place little value on supernatural explanations or on secret wisdom. Instead their orientation towards everyday reality makes matters of ethics, justice, honesty, and fellowship central.

In addition to plot and setting, Hopewell concentrates upon characterization of a congregation. The concept of character includes both the social profile of a congregation and its heritage. But Hopewell employs the concept of character to bring one more dimension of congregational life into view, the moral one. By asking "What is the character of this congregation?" he directs attention to the values, the "preferred behavioral tone," the ethos, the "corporate integrity" of a congregation. In contrast to the purpose of worldview analysis which "treats what people suspect is going on," emphasis on character isolates "what they wish would go on."

One especially fruitful way to gain insight into a congregation's character is to conduct a ritual inventory of its life. By ritual, Hopewell means "repetitive actions that have more than utilitarian significance, such as ways of greeting, celebration, negotiation, intimacy, and grief." The most obvious types of congregational ritual are "rites of passage." These occur around significant moments of human transition, such as birth, coming of age, marriage, and death. In these moments of profound personal and communal change, rituals are used to express the core values and beliefs of a culture in the hope that a new appropriation of them will take place. In a place of worship, these rituals would include baptism, circumcision, confirmation, bar and bat mitzvahs, weddings, reception of new members, funerals or memorial services, and ordination or installation of clergy. At such times congregations summarize and powerfully condense into ritual language their understandings of who they are and who they want to be.

In addition to rites of passage there is another cluster of rituals which Hopewell calls "rites of intensification." These rites are celebrated not so much for the purpose of interpreting dramatic changes in individual or corporate life as they are performed to renew and intensify commitment to a congregation's great and little traditions. The special occasions of a congregation's yearly life — Rosh Hashanah, Yom Kippur, Christmas, Easter, The Lord's Supper, Thanksgiving, Memorial Day — are examples, but so are Founders' Days, annual church suppers and sales, coffee hours, and congregational meetings. In such events and liturgical occasions dimensions of congregational style and valuing are expressed.

To balance the characterization of a congregation Hopewell also encourages participant-observers to pay attention to the "underlife" of a congregation, its "street wisdom." By paying attention to how things actually get done, by noting the types of behavior that are reinforced and those that are rebuked in various informal settings within the congregation it becomes possible to discern its "etiquette" and preferred style. Attention to these informal realms of congregational practice can add nuance to the character sketch the historian is drawing.

Hopewell's approach can be a provocative sensitizer for congregational historians. It encourages searching many levels of congregational life for overlooked aspects of significant behavior. And it asks many questions which can assist those who wish to identify the particular genius of a congregation. But the method also has its dangers. His typology of world views, for example, can easily be used in a heavy-handed manner which obscures the pluralism that exists within congregations. The richness of individual stories within a congregation can be lost in the quest for congregational character. A comic congregation may in fact have members with tragic or ironic stories to tell.

 'In addition, his efforts to arrive at the particular story of a congregation can unintentionally freeze that story at a particular moment in its life, a moment that some have called the "specious present." If analysis of the present story of a congregation is all that needs to be done then there is no reason for readers to move beyond this chapter. Yet congregational history aspires to a story that moves beyond current visions of the past. It aims at a sense of what actually happened — which can be very different from the short term memories Hopewell unearths.

This book seeks to help congregational historians become aware of how congregations paradoxically stay the same and change over time. Part of the process of change in a congregation's life is the way its story develops and the way its mood, worldview, and ethos change. Thus a congregation's story is continually being edited and revised — even in those moments when the strongest appeals to continuity and tradition are made.

Congregational historians therefore can learn a great deal from Hopewell's questions and approaches to their subject. His pressure to find a story that can comprehend all of the multifaceted reality present within a congregation is one they must feel. But to his set of concerns they must bring the historian's sensitivity to ongoing plot development and to the human diversity present within each congregation. The tension between contemporary generalizations about worldview on the one hand and particular instances and anomalies that shift as time passes on the other presents rich possibilities for history writing.

Chapter 3 considers the nuts and bolts of congregational history which can relativize first impressions. Names, dates, places, and events — the essential raw materials which accumulate over the years — help balance first impressions. In many cases plundering the archives of a congregation will help relativize a current congregational understanding. Frequently, the historian will turn up evidence that "we have not always done it this way," or that "things were different back then." The three detours of this chapter were taken in order to sharpen awareness of the preconceptions that people often take with them into historical research. They also serve the purpose of raising a set of questions in the congregational historian's mind that points to dynamics and patterns present within the congregation's current reality. Such questions can make seemingly trivial data in dusty file folders come to life because some aspect of the present situation has put a new interest or concern in the historian's mind. At the same time the data of the past will do its own subtle reshaping of the initial set of questions posed by the congregational historian. This lively reciprocal interchange between a congregation's past and present is one of the keys to an invigorating process of history writing. But before turning to the materials and questions more traditionally associated with the historical task, it is important to consider one more aspect of a congregation's present circumstances: its social context.

For Further Reading

St. Jerome's Letter #107 is quoted in John Bartlett, *Familiar Quotations*, Fifteenth Edition (Boston: Little, Brown and Company, 1980), p. 128.

Otto von Simson provides an excellent scholarly study of what lies behind the great religious edifices of the middle ages in *The Gothic Cathedral* (Princeton, New Jersey: Princeton University Press, 1962). See especially pp. xx, xiv, 89.

Melvin D. Williams' *Community in a Black Pentecostal Church: An Anthropological Study* (Pittsburgh: University of Pittsburgh Press, 1974) gives a useful example of the riches to be gained by employing the techniques of participant-observation. See especially pp. 3-4, 29, 36, 38, 61-2, 73, 76, 81, and 144.

James M. Gustafson discusses the multidimensional character of congregations in *Treasure in Earthen Vessels: The Church as a Human Community* (Chicago: The University of Chicago Press, 1961). The lengthy quotation is from p. 5.

Those interested in a more complete explanation of James F. Hopewell's model should consult the author's "The Jovial Church: Narrative in Local Church Life," in Carl S. Dudley, editor, *Building Effective Ministry: Theory and Practice in the Local Church* (San Francisco: Harper & Row, Publishers, 1983), pp. 68-83, and "Identity," in Jackson W. Carroll, Carl S. Dudley and William McKinney, editors, *Handbook for Congregational Studies* (Nashville: Abingdon Press, 1986), pp. 21-38. For Hopewell's most comprehensive statement of his perspective see *Congregation: Stories and Structures* (Philadelphia: Fortress Press, 1987).

Relating First Impressions to Historical Inquiry

Recently sociologist R. Stephen Warner described the ways in which firsthand observations of contemporary congregational life combined with more traditional historical research to produce a richer portrait of the Presbyterian church he was studying:

"I went to a meeting of the session and was offered access to the church archives by the clerk of that body. . . . I also knew that I would have to seek out those — some whose names I was to learn from the archives — who had ceased participating in the church. I had to dig deeper into the background of Antioch Fellowship. In short, I must become more the historian. I did not cease my watching and hobnobbing on my return to Mendocino in October, but I added many hours of work in the church office and sought out those who were strategic but less convenient interviewees.

The archives turned out to be a gold mine. . . . Above all, the minutes of session, which I eventually read carefully for 1957 through 1982, were indispensable.

The minutes recorded the officers elected at the annual congregational meetings and their subsequent records of service; church members added to the rolls and whence they came; members deleted and deceased; dates of service of pastors; and a careful, literate, and discreet record of deliberations of the session itself. . . . Without my interviews and my own observation of a session meeting, I would have found it impossible to decipher many cryptic references. Nothing was sharply worded, all the hard edges of controversy having been sanded down by the clerks in the four weeks between meetings. But history was there to be read between the lines."

New Wine in Old Wineskins: Evangelicals and Liberals in a Small-Town Church (Berkeley: University of California Press, 1988), pp. 78-9.

·2·

Creating a Landscape

AS FASCINATING AS PLACES OF WORSHIP ARE IN THEIR interior variety, there is much more that the historian needs to learn about them. Later chapters consider the dimensions of a congregation's history that can be discovered by digging in a church's archives or through investigating a denomination's, a town's, or a region's history. But this chapter's purpose is to call attention to the significance of the terrain which surrounds the congregation. It is important to become aware of the ways in which a congregation relates to its social context before setting out to explore the preceding chapter's tantalizing leads and turning to the more conventional tasks of history writing. Just as historians need to make use of current experience in their research they also must be sensitive to the effects of a congregation's location — both geographical and sociological — upon its life, past and present. The net result should be a more colorful, insightful, and lively portrait of the congregation.

A synagogue's or parish's terrain includes the climate, topography, neighborhood, economic environment, and social niche which constitute its setting. As the historian takes note of these contextual factors a landscape emerges which will give palpability to a particular portrait.

Locating a Congregation

One can begin this task by working in either of two directions. The first is to proceed from the inside out. This approach places the historian on the front step of the congregation. From there a mental (perhaps actual) map can be drawn that stretches out to the neighborhood, community, region, nation, etc. The second direction lofts

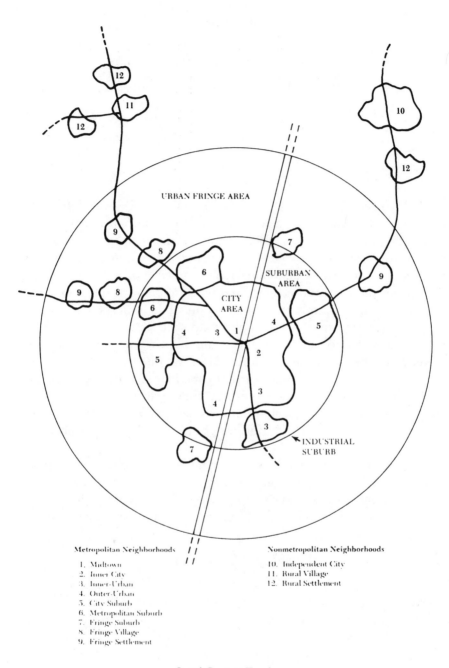

URBAN FRINGE AREA

SUBURBAN
AREA

CITY
AREA

INDUSTRIAL
SUBURB

Metropolitan Neighborhoods

1. Midtown
2. Inner City
3. Inner-Urban
4. Outer-Urban
5. City Suburb
6. Metropolitan Suburb
7. Fringe Suburb
8. Fringe Village
9. Fringe Settlement

Nonmetropolitan Neighborhoods

10. Independent City
11. Rural Village
12. Rural Settlement

Social Context Typology

congregational historians to an imaginary vantage point in our earth's stratosphere. From there a succession of maps can be drawn which help place a congregation in the earth's ecology, in a hemisphere, climactic zone, terrain, nation, region, town, neighborhood, etc. This outside-in approach mimics the photographer with the telephoto lens who keeps taking pictures of the same object, but zooms in a bit closer with each click of the shutter.

Both approaches remind historians of the fundamental role a congregation's ecology plays in its story. A location in southern Mississippi will result in a different type of story than one in northern Alaska. Desert terrain shapes a congregation's life in different ways than a flood plain does, or a mountain range. In later chapters attention is given to a Boston temple and an Idaho church. Their different social locations shape very distinctive stories. To ignore the social difference is to leave out a key ingredient. Individual historians will choose one route into their congregation's context over another. But an occasional employment of the other vantage point may help bring unnoticed features of a landscape into view.

The map on the facing page provides a helpful point of departure for thinking about the more immediate environment of a congregation, which is the main concern of this chapter. Prepared by a seasoned congregation watcher this map actually proposes a way of classifying congregations on the basis of their geography. While Douglas A. Walrath would not go so far as to claim that you know everything about a congregation by identifying where it fits on this map, he does suggest that congregations take on different characteristics in each of the eleven different zones he has identified.

Assume for a moment that you are standing at ground zero on Professor Walrath's map. You are at the center of a city, in the middle of his map. You notice that the important demarcations are between city, suburb, and fringe zones. This way of drawing the map recognizes that the modern city is one of the basic features of American life. In many ways relationship to one of our land's major cities, whether that be one of proximity or distance, defines the contours of distinct patterns of life. The high-rise dweller in midtown follows a work-play-socialize rhythm quite different from the farmer in a rural settlement. Congregations which seek to minister to people in these very different contexts must mesh their programs and styles with the distinctive ways of life fostered by particular environments.

So important is this contextual factor in Walrath's estimation that he argues that each type of region will have a "characteristic" church. In the inner city he expects to find struggling, perhaps subsidized congregations. The metropolitan suburban church tends to be oriented to the needs of nuclear families and might focus its resources on running a parish school. Churches in rural villages frequently suffer from loss of membership due to migration of members toward the city. Rural settlement churches, those which are most remote from the city, tend to hold their own on membership charts due in part to the reverse migration of people seeking escape from the pressures of the city.

We need not consider here each of Walrath's eleven congregational types. Nor for our purposes is it important that we agree with this mapmaker's characterizations of typical churches for specific contexts. (Readers who wish to know more about particular types are invited to consult his essay.) But congregational historians do need to take seriously his claim that there are distinct social contexts and that those contexts play important shaping roles in the life of any congregation.

In addition to this device for classifying congregational contexts Professor Walrath proposes categories to assist in determining a congregation's "social position" within a particular environment. By asking whether a congregation sits in a *dominant, subordinate,* or *exclusive* posture over against its community, another aspect of its relationship to its context comes into view.

Dominant churches can be recognized by paying attention to matters of size, address, age, and prestige. These congregations tend to be "First" churches or synagogues, they are viewed as leading institutions within the community. Often they reveal their social position through impressive architecture and prominent locations on village greens or main streets.

Subordinate churches, on the other hand, are viewed as the "other" church in town. These "Second," "Third," and "Fourth" churches tend to be latecomers in the community and often occupy less strategic spots on its horizon. While they often overlap with the dominant congregations in terms of appeal to mainstream constituencies, they are not perceived as the community's powerful churches.

Quite different from these types is the *exclusive* congregation. These

Chicago's Fourth Presbyterian Church occupies a dominant position in its community.

institutions do not aspire to community-wide inclusiveness. Instead, they select one group within a community and customize their efforts accordingly. Examples of such churches or synagogues are those that serve a distinct ethnic group.

But in the last several decades customized congregations for apartment dwellers, gay people, charismatic Christians, and social activists have all found niches in the American religious environment. These congregations may be less visible to the general public than the first two types. Perhaps the most pronounced example of this type of congregation is the kind which embodies what Robert S. Ellwood, Jr., called the spirituality of the cave. This form of religious life is quite different from that of the temple, where mainstream people gather to worship. Cave religion takes place in out of the way places, some of them intentionally concealed. Many of the new religions which swept across the United

St. James the Lesser Episcopal Church in a nearby suburb sits in a more subordinant setting.

Mt. Carmel Missionary Baptist Church in another part of the city blends into its community's architecture so well that most passersby will fail to notice it.

States in the sixties and seventies fit this most exclusive form. So do earlier Pentecostal expressions in this century. A drive down a city street can often reveal very unpretentious storefront congregations — some willing to be seen, others seeking anonymity. Unless they pose a threat — real or imagined to community well being and custom — neither cavelike variety commands the kind of social attention of the dominant temples or churches associated with mainline religion.

How useful are such "social locating" categories? Historians can welcome them as useful eye openers to important elements in a congregational story. Something as humdrum as a parish's zip code can provide useful information by pointing to an environment which may be economically upscale or the opposite. But, as usual, historians have to be careful in using such distinctions. Contexts do not tell the whole story. Why, for example, would a white Baptist church in a South Carolina suburb welcome blacks into its congregation while another Baptist church in a similar context in Texas excludes them? The answer will not be found by paying attention only to matters of geography. Instead a careful correlating of the inner life of a congregation with its context will have to be developed.

One more caution about social location needs to be raised. Historians are always looking for how things change and stay the same as time passes. Therefore, it is important to note how a congregation can stay in one geographic area and still experience major shifts in social location. Chicago's LaSalle Street Church, for instance, has seen its neighborhood change numerous times. In the 1830s a group of German evangelicals settled on their city's north side. As the years slipped by they were followed by Swedes, Italians, Japanese Americans, Appalachian whites, Puerto Ricans, blacks, and yuppies in successive demographic waves across this part of the city. With each change in context, the congregation changed. Yet in some ways it retained an identity in the midst of all the upheaval.

Most congregations will not have as many dramatic contextual shifts as LaSalle Street Church. But historians will want to watch for more subtle social and economic shifts and look for how they affect their particular congregations.

Mission Stances

Congregations are not merely passive pawns on a contextual chessboard. Or at least they do not have to be. As strong an influence as environment is, it seldom is powerful enough to keep congregations from

LaSalle Street Church, Chicago, Illinois.

influencing their contexts in both subtle and dramatic ways. Those ways come into view when questions are asked about the congregation's mission beyond its walls. What style does the congregation set within its community? What stance does it take toward the world beyond it? What distinguishes the congregation's identity from that of its community? The goal of the congregational historian is to discover a complete congregational identity — one that reflects community influences without being overwhelmed by them.

St. Margaret's Catholic Church (a pseudonym for a downtown Hartford, Connecticut, parish) illustrates this point. This Hispanic congregation is one of more than four hundred churches in the greater Hartford area. Located in the inner city it ministers to the poorest of Hartford's citizens. Its eight hundred adults and children worship in a seventy-three-year-old edifice built by German Catholics. St. Margaret's retained its original ethnic identity until its neighborhood changed in the late 1940s. By 1956 waves of black and Hispanic newcomers had so altered the social context that St. Margaret's was designated a "national Hispanic parish." Now the church's white brick sanctuary finds itself surrounded by heavy industry, boarded up storefronts, and run-down housing.

This place of worship reflects its local circumstances in many ways. The parish celebrated its last English mass in 1981. On Festival days one is more likely to hear the sounds of the cuatro (a double-stringed guitar) than the organ cherished by the Germans. Indicators such as these reveal the powerful impact of demographic changes upon a congregation. They also make appealing a type of social determinism which sees little possibility for a congregation to create an identity distinct from its social milieu. Once we have located St. Margaret's on Professor Walrath's map, this line of reasoning suggests, we know exactly what to expect.

Yet a second look at St. Margaret's suggests something else. How can we account for the fact that in July 1982, when President Reagan came to town, forty-five of St. Margaret's members participated in a public demonstration against his nuclear war and poverty policies? Or that when gang activity became especially ominous the parish's priests and deacons led a group which patrolled nearby streets for two weeks? Why has this congregation chosen an activist posture in its context when other city churches send no members into the streets to protest or protect? The answers may well come from religious beliefs and traditions of mission with roots in a past much older than St. Margaret's. Did the Germans have an aggressive mission tradition which has outlived them? Did priests import this activism from experiences in seminary or Third World? Has there been an active lay leadership in this parish which has always felt responsibility for the neighborhood?

Or when looking at the programs conducted by this parish how do we explain its commitment to seek out the needy of the community and help them? What is it saying about itself as it conducts Head-Start programs for pre-school children, runs its *Rio Piedras* tutorial center for elementary and secondary children, or sponsors a summer educational

program which fills the empty time of inner city children with meaningful activity? What can we learn about this congregation from the fact
that it has chosen to respond to local housing needs with its own
Roberto Clemente Housing Corporation which simultaneously employs
young people to renovate buildings and makes available low cost
housing?

Concrete congregational relationships to the community can be
discerned in each of these activities and many others such as support for
the neighborhood's soup kitchen and thrift shop. While the church's
social context clearly has presented St. Margaret's with major social
realities like poverty and ethnicity, that context has been affected by the
church's aggressive understanding of its mission. St. Margaret's did not
have to respond to the problems faced by inner-city youngsters with all
the programs it has created. Rather, some internal quality, whether it be
the vision of its priests, the commitment of its people, or a tradition of
community involvement must be identified to account for this congregation's response to its environment.

The determination of a congregation's mission orientation, or stance
towards the world, may seem to be an elusive task. Long-time association
with a parish or synagogue can blur the boundaries between congregation and community. *Mission* can come to mean the exotic actions of a
congregation — sending a Bible translator to Nicaragua or supporting a
water project in the Sudan. On the other hand, this matter may seem
self-evident. Strong traditions about mission, reaching back to prophets
like Micah who counselled Israel to "do justice and love mercy" (6:8)
may make historians confident they know exactly where to look.

The insights developed by three sociologists of religion can sharpen
our vision. David A. Roozen, William McKinney, and Jackson W.
Carroll spent several years studying the congregations of Hartford,
Connecticut. The description of St. Margaret's Church is derived from
their research. But more instructive for our purposes than their case
study of St. Margaret's is the typology, or classification system they
developed. In their judgment congregations assume one of four mission
orientations to the world around them. They can be *activist, civic,
sanctuary,* or *evangelistic* in their stances. While most congregations
showed evidence of multiple stances, these sociologists felt that a
dominant orientation usually emerged in each institution. A fault line
ran through their study. Congregations tended to fall on one side or the

other of a this-worldly/other-worldly distinction. That is, some congregations were primarily concerned with helping people live in the everyday world while others placed primary emphasis on the world to come. Activist and civic orientations were found on the this-worldly side. Sanctuary and evangelistic ones existed on the other.

These scholars made their determination of a congregation's mission stance by administering a carefully designed questionnaire which examined members' opinions on public issues like housing, world hunger, crime, and homosexuality. They also examined varieties of congregational involvement in outreach programs. Did this particular church or synagogue conduct a senior citizens program, pray about social justice issues, operate a parochial school, or let outside groups use its place of worship? On the basis of answers to these and many other questions a congregation was placed in one of the four orientation categories.

I am not suggesting that congregational historians need to administer the kinds of questionnaires developed by these scholars. (Although they may find some useful questions for their own work by reviewing the types of questions asked.) Instead I want to suggest a softer use of their categories. As these scholars readily admit, few congregations will be pure examples of one particular type. Rather, most will be "mixed" institutions with some dimensions of two or more types existing side by side. Nonetheless, by examining a particular congregation in light of these four ideal stances a historian can bring another side of its story to light.

St. Margaret's, for example, is placed by these scholars into the first, or activist type. That is, this kind of church focuses upon the "here and now" world as its main arena of concern. Activist churches seek to make corporate responses to community needs and view "the achievement of a more just and humane society" as one of their primary reasons for being. These congregations are not satisfied with spiritually well-prepared individuals who participate in the world's crises. Instead, they attempt to make corporate, collective contributions to those situations.

St. Margaret's distinctiveness becomes more apparent when placed against a background which includes the other types. The other major variety of this-worldly congregations is the civic church. This kind of congregation wants to improve life in this world, but tends to be more accepting of the dominant structures of society. Rather than confront as St. Margaret's did with its protest marches and alternative educational

and housing systems civic congregations seek to educate and contribute
to a community's cultural life. Less emphasis is placed upon corporate
action. Instead, these congregations are places where individuals can
prepare to make their own social contributions. As a forum for the
consideration of a community's needs a civic church puts a premium on
qualities like civility and tolerance, virtues which may seem to be vices
by holders of some of the other orientations.

Quite different from St. Margaret's orientation are those which fall on
the other-worldly side of the fault line. Sanctuary churches, for example,
become places of refuge from a world that is basically seen as hopeless.
The sense here is not that of the political activism of the recent
"sanctuary movement" in the U.S. Instead, emphasis is placed on
creating a unified inner world where individual lives of decency and
uprightness can be cultivated. Little effort will be made to change the
community by a sanctuary church, as these scholars employ the term. Its
interest in its larger community will consist primarily in supporting a
social system which allows the congregation's life to go on with
minimum interference.

Evangelistic congregations, while sharing primary concern for the
world to come with sanctuary churches, are more aggressive in public life
than their other-worldly cousins. These congregations actively seek to
share their message of salvation or truth with those outside their walls.
Thus one might find members of an evangelistic church in the streets
alongside the members of St. Margaret's. But while St. Margaret's
members may be seeking structural change in society, the evangelistic
congregation members will be seeking to draw people to their message.

While an arbitrary imposition of these mission orientations can result
in a caricature of a congregation rather than an authentic portrait,
consideration of the questions beneath the types can open up major
lines of research. These orientations raise questions about basic relationships between a congregation and its context. They nudge us to find out
what the community has thought about a particular synagogue or
parish. How has the congregation been portrayed in community
newspapers and local histories? As an activist place or as a sanctuary-
minded group of people? What social programs are seen by insiders and
outsiders alike as typical for this congregation? And why? And what
about the relationships created by individual members of a congregation? What interdenominational, paracongregational, secular, and ad

hoc groups do they belong to? In what ways do these associations allow the congregation to reach beyond its walls and into the lives of community members?

The examples of La Salle Street Church and St. Margaret's provide vivid reminders of the role of context in a congregation's history. Clearly, landscapes change and with them, congregations do too. Thus wise historians will not allow themselves to be preoccupied with current environmental realities. Instead, they will take social context questions with them as they examine the traces of a church's or synagogue's past. They will also seek to discern relationships between a congregation's responses to its context and its fundamental beliefs and traditions.

For Further Reading

Douglas A. Walrath developed his typologies in "Types of Small Congregations and Their Implications for Planning," in Jackson W. Carroll, editor, *Small Churches are Beautiful* (San Francisco: Harper & Row, 1977), pp. 33-61.

Robert S. Ellwood, Jr., opens up a realm of religious life unknown to most of us in *Alternative Altars: Unconventional and Eastern Spirituality in America* (Chicago: The University of Chicago Press, 1979). The distinction between spirituality of the cave and that of the temple is made on pp. 4-6.

James and Marti Hefley, *The Church that Takes on Trouble: The Story of Chicago's La Salle Street Church* (Elgin, IL: David C. Cook Publishing Co., 1976) is a congregational history that gives special attention to the impact of a changing social context. See especially pp. 24-6.

David A. Roozen, William McKinney, and Jackson W. Carroll's *Varieties of Religious Presence: Mission in Public Life* (New York: The Pilgrim Press, 1984) goes into much greater detail on each of the four mission stances summarized in this chapter. The book's collection of case studies that exemplify each type are also instructive. See especially pp. 32-6, 160-75.

· 3 ·

Indispensable Questions

NO CONSCIENTIOUS CONGREGATIONAL HISTORIAN wants his or her work to resemble a personal scrapbook filled with a hodge-podge of unrelated souvenirs that make little sense to anyone except the original collector. Few of us wish to read or write books that look like religious phone directories with unending lists of names or expanded versions of congregational minutes which record every detail so completely that it becomes impossible to separate the important from the insignificant.

Here it is important to face up to one of the great temptations of history writing — the desire to use every tidbit discovered in the painstaking work of mining sources for their treasures. The type of congregational history writing this book seeks to foster has a very different end-product in mind than a book which looks like someone emptied a too-full mental vacuum cleaner on its pages.

While historians depend on sources for their work, they dare not simply pile up mountains of data and then unload them on the unsuspecting reader. Instead, the historian, like a good detective, must become adept at finding the essential clues which can contribute to an overall interpretation or story. The telling incident, the representative person, the critical event, the new idea, the powerful but unrecognized process — these are the targets of historical investigation. They provide the primary building blocks out of which the historian will construct a narrative. They allow the historian the freedom to choose which facts will be included in the final draft and which ones will be left out.

How do we find the important pieces of data which give shape to the compelling and informative narrative? Part of the answer is to think like a journalist. A good newspaper reporter always approaches an assignment — whether it is the assassination of a president or the announcement of the latest change in hemlines — with the same set of questions. Who? What? When? Where? Why? How? These are primary means for sifting through piles of data. They are the questions that set people on the trail of new sources of information when old ones leave either doubt in the mind or gaping holes in understanding. They can also send an inquirer scurrying back to a previously examined source when a new clue suggests that what has been assumed may not be the complete or final word.

These questions can serve the congregational historian as well. The credibility of a historical interpretation depends upon how well its generalizations are supported by answers to the journalist's questions. They will help the historian supply concreteness, detail, vividness, and distinctiveness to a particular synagogue's or church's story. They can, if organized and ruled by a plot or theme, keep individual congregational histories from dreary sameness and tedium.

How would the journalist's questions work for congregational historians? Here are some sample ways to focus them on congregations:

WHO —
1. Who were the people who created this congregation?
2. Who have been its leaders? Its quiet pewsitters? Its discontented members?
3. Who have been the people who joined the congregation?
4. Who left and why?
5. Who have been the people who wanted to change things in the congregation's life? Who wanted to keep things the same?
6. Who have been the spiritual people in the congregation? Who have served as its moral consciences? Who have been the status seekers and the power brokers?
7. Who have been the congregation's neighbors? Who has the congregation sought for membership? Who has the congregation sought to keep out of its midst?
8. Who have shaped special interests of the congregation?
9. Who transmitted the congregation's identity and traditions to the next generation — and to newcomers?

WHAT —

1. What did the founders set out to achieve when they formed this congregation? What have new members sought here?
2. What have been the congregation's official reasons for being, its official beliefs, its stances on moral, social, and theological issues?
3. What questions or problems have caused conflict in the congregation? What has been this congregation's style for dealing with controversy? What means has it used for resolving conflict?
4. What self-image has this congregation maintained?
5. What have been this congregation's distinctive customs, traditions, and values?
6. What has this congregation been especially proud of? What has it been embarrassed by?
7. What have been key turning points in the life of the congregation? What were the factors that shaped those events? What happened in their aftermath?
8. What has this congregation believed about God, society, itself, the individual?
9. What have been its greatest challenges? Achievements? Disasters? Failures?
10. What has held this congregation together? What threatened to pull it apart?
11. What heritage has it treasured? What tradition(s) has it claimed? What values has it esteemed of which it is unaware?

WHEN —

1. When did this congregation begin?
2. When has it experienced dramatic changes in membership?
3. When has it met for worship? For decision? For service? For social action?
4. When has it experienced controversy and turmoil?
5. When has it taken new directions? When has it reaffirmed old ways of doing things?
6. When has it been ahead of society as prophet? When has it lagged behind as preserver of the status quo?
7. When have significant changes in leadership taken place?
8. When have new groups formed in the life of this congregation?

9. When has this congregation celebrated significant milestones in its life?
10. When will/did the life of this congregation come to an end?

WHERE —
1. Where did this congregation's members come from?
2. Where have new members come from?
3. Where has it built its buildings?
4. Where has it placed its priorities?
5. Where have lay leaders and clergy come from?
6. Where have members gone when they left this congregation?
7. Where have congregation members spent their time?
8. Where has it located its mission?
9. Where has this congregation turned for help or for resources for its ministry?
10. Where have new ideas come from in the life of this congregation?
11. Where have the congregation's most powerful competitors — both secular and religious — been found?

WHY —
1. Why did this congregation come into being?
2. Why has it chosen the particular building design(s) it has? Why did it locate on this particular piece of earth?
3. Why have new leaders appeared on the scene? Why have old ones disappeared?
4. Why have this congregation's controversies or conflicts emerged when, where, and how they did?
5. Why have people continued/failed to join this congregation?
6. Why has this congregation made its significant changes — in worship, in organizational life, in membership requirements, in sense of mission, in sense of identity?
7. Why does this congregation handle its economic resources the way it does?
8. Why have people stayed in this congregation?
9. Why have young people dropped out at certain times in their lives and why have others seemed to join at particular moments in their life cycles?

10. Why have these people continued to gather, week in and week out?

HOW —

1. How has this congregation expressed its fundamental beliefs in specific practices?
2. How have membership patterns changed/stayed the same over the years?
3. How has power been distributed in this congregation?
4. How has this congregation made its decisions?
5. How has it spent its money?
6. How has it determined if it is succeeding or failing?
7. How has it responded to changes in society, denomination, neighborhood?
8. How has change been perceived in the congregation?
9. How has this congregation expressed its specialness?
10. How has this congregation told its story to new and younger members? How has it educated them or formed them spiritually?
11. How has this congregation expressed itself artistically, musically, theologically, socially?

It is important to remember that historians are more than reporters. While they may ask questions like those listed here, they have a distinctive interest which sets them apart from journalists. Above all, they are interested in the problems posed by the passing of time. They want to know what happens at this moment, then at the next. But more than mere chronology, historians are concerned to discover which things endure, which things change, and which things disappear as time passes.

·4·

Building Blocks

ALTHOUGH THEY OFTEN TAKE CREATIVE LEAPS OF imagination, historians do not create their stories out of thin air. They must have sources, and those sources determine in fundamental ways what each historian has to say. In this chapter we move to the historian's homefield, the remains of the past. Stimulated by first impressions and landscape features, and armed with a lively set of questions, it is time to mine the sources.

One way to help historians identify the sources of information which may provide answers to their questions is to list categories recognizable to any historian, no matter what he or she is studying. According to Professors David E. Kyvig and Myron A. Marty historical "traces" can be classified as follows:

> a. Immaterial traces are intangible but clearly apparent remnants from the past, such as institutions, customs, traditions, beliefs, principles, practices, superstitions, legends, and language.

> b. Material traces, easier to grasp, consist of objects, things, artifacts of the past, products of human doings.

> c. Written traces come in many varieties. Some may be handwritten, such as letters, diaries, journals, and manuscripts. Newspapers, books, magazines, and pamphlets are printed traces.

> d. The fourth kind of trace is both a real thing, having tangible, sensory presence, and a representation of something else. For want of a better term, we call this a "representational" trace. The best example is a photograph.

Kyvig and Marty also remind us that there is a difference between the intentional source, prepared in order that later generations might encounter it, and the unpremeditated source, which falls into the discoverer's hands by accident. Examples of the former are presidential libraries and official documents. Examples of the latter are the scribbled notes in the margin of a private memo or the materials found in a garbage dump outside a town wall.

Each of these two types has a different kind of message. Intentional sources disclose what people wanted others to believe about what they were doing. Unpremeditated sources on the other hand provide insights to hidden motives (often from the actors themselves) and taken-for-granted aspects of life which may shed much light upon the public side of people's behavior. These hidden or taken-for-granted elements often shape events in profound ways — perhaps more powerfully than those that are highly visible. A church may declare in an official resolution that its reason for moving to the suburbs is to evangelize an unchurched population. It may never mention the new ethnic group that is changing the face of the old neighborhood. But a member's diary could reveal the fear. History that is built on only one of these types of sources runs the risk of being skewed. One may end up with either propaganda or gossip if the two are not carefully related.

At the same time Kyvig and Marty suggest several helpful rules of thumb for weighing our sources. First, historians should determine the relationship between a particular source and the event which stands behind it. When dealing with written documents ask "How close is this source to the event it is describing or explaining?" Is it from an eyewitness or from someone who is telling the story second or third hand? Was it written the day the event occured or fifty years later when someone sat down and reminisced? What point of view is taken by this source — was the author a supporter or an opponent, an optimist or a pessimist, an insider or an outsider?

Second, historians need to be careful to ask questions which the sources can answer. They always need to be cautious about reading their own agendas into the data they are examining.

Third, Kyvig and Marty caution us about drawing inferences from the absence of traces. Instead, search for identifiable relationships between traces and events.

Fourth, historians need to be scrupulous about any source's

authenticity. More than one historian has been misled by the spurious document or the fabricated explanation. Is there convincing internal and external proof that this source is what it claims to be?

Fifth, care should be taken to keep events and the sources which testify to them in their proper context. An isolated source can support many interpretations. A source placed in its original context becomes more precise and disclosive.

Finally inferences about events should be expressed in language of probability rather than absolute certainty. Because we do not deal with instant replays of events but the recollections of people who have lapses of memory, partial understandings, and mixed motives we need to remind readers and ourselves that while we try to determine "what actually happened" our reconstructions are, at best, only approximations.

Rather than continue this theoretical discussion of sources, I now wish to invite the reader to take a mental stroll with me through the archives of one particular congregation. Noticing what kinds of traces one congregation has saved from its past can help readers to identify sources within the place of worship they are studying.

First United Methodist Church, Evanston, Illinois.

The congregation I have selected is First United Methodist Church of Evanston, Illinois. Founded in 1854 and strategically placed in what was once one of Methodism's northern strongholds, First United is definitely *not* a representative congregation. In fact everything about it testifies to this congregation's distinctiveness, its specialness — including its impressive archives.

This congregation was the first church founded in one of Chicago's first suburbs. It grew up alongside Northwestern University and Garrett Biblical Institute, two powerful Methodist institutions built and run by many of the same people who belonged to First United. Its buildings were designed by architects with national reputations, its clergy were frequently rated as among the top five or ten preachers in the United States. Its ushers wore swallow tail coats until the 1960s and the people who rented the congregation's pews early in this century were among the Who's Who of Chicago's prestigious North Shore. Known for its lavish New Year's Eve parties, host to so many dinners that it ran its own commissary with a salaried staff, site of one of the earliest nationally televised Christmas Eve services, and cohost with Northwestern University of the only meeting of the World Council of Churches to take place on U.S. soil, this church has been one of our nation's most prominent mainline congregations since the time of its founding in 1854. It seems worlds removed from Zion Church in Pittsburgh or St. Margaret's Parish in Hartford — and from many other Methodist churches, for that matter. And in many ways — those ways that make congregational history writing so interesting — it is!

So why start here? The answer becomes apparent when we begin to stroll into this congregation's rich collection of sources. Lest we fail to make use of the perspectives called for in chapter 1 let me pause to take note of the splendid building which houses this congregation. Built in 1911 and expanded in 1930 the church expresses the master vision of architect Thomas Eddy Tallmadge. Its neo-Gothic tower, stained glass, and wood and stone carvings express a great deal about what the members and leaders of First Church valued. Cathedral-like in style it presides over its Evanston neighborhood and quietly proclaims a congregation's self-understanding regarding matters of community status and refinement. To draw on an insight from chapter 2, the way this building fits in its landscape indicates that this is a dominant congregation.

First Methodist Episcopal Church.
PEW RENTALS.

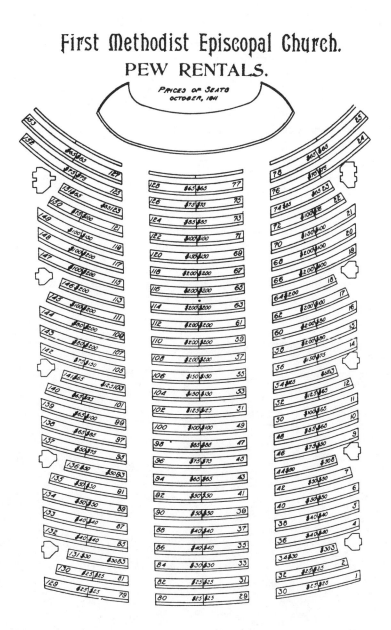

Sometimes one document can reveal a great deal. This chart points to First United's primary economic strategy during an earlier period in history. It also reveals assumptions about social order and status within the congregation.

The wood carvings in the reredos which surrounds the altar of the church proclaim the centrality of Jesus as they draw the eye to scenes of his life and his resurrection. Another reredos located in the Ernest Fremont Tittle Chapel, however, is surprisingly secular. Featuring the figures of Plato, Newton, Aristotle, Dante, Michaelangelo, Justinian, and a workingman named *Toil*, this slightly less prominent group of carvings suggests that members of this congregation also wanted to embrace and sanctify much of the worldly, the human — philosophy, science, rhetoric, literature, art, law, and common labor.

In less than an hour of strolling through this main "material source," one finds a significant question raised in wood and stone. First Church wanted to keep Jesus central in its life and at the same time be open to all the strivings of the human spirit. How did this church deal with its dual orientation? Whether or not this sculpted puzzle turns out to be the best question to shape this congregation's history can only be determined after other sources have been examined, but a congregational historian can miss a great deal if he or she is in too great a hurry to get to the files.

Pictures like this one can give specificity to assumptions about a congregation's style and character.

Reredos of main altar, First United Methodist Church.

Let's continue the stroll. Elsewhere in First Church's hallways one finds other pieces of material that raise questions. The plaque in the narthex commemorating the opening worship service of the World Council of Churches, held on August 15, 1954, should flag a major topic for future investigation. So should several prominent reminders of the pivotal ministry of Ernest Freemont Tittle — his ashes in the floor of the chapel that bears his name, and the plaques commemorating his ministry.

Reredos behind altar in the Ernest Fremont Tittle Chapel.

But traces of other key people in the life of the congregation can be found as well. A stained glass window in the church depicts Frances Willard, one of the great women leaders of temperance and other reform movements during the Progressive Era and a member of this congregation. There are portraits of Methodism's founder John Wesley, Robert M. Hatfield (an early pastor), and Tallmadge the architect. Rooms of the building are named for parishioners and pieces of furniture and key mementos express the grandeur of early twentieth-century life on the North Shore. Such a stroll should leave one well prepared for opening the door into First Church's archives.

In a dim and completely unnoteworthy corner of First Church's basement one comes to the archives. Access is limited to those who have permission from an official of the congregation and use is monitored by the congregation's archivist who unlocks the room at announced hours. None of the archival materials may be removed from the room (a policy which helps to ensure the survival of the congregation's historical

Procession of Delegates entering Opening Worship Service of the World Council of Churches, August 15, 1954. One of First United's ushers can be seen in formal attire at the upper right of the picture.

treasures). Quickly the archivist orients the inquirer. As readers follow her tour of the shelves and file cabinets they can begin to prepare their own check lists for the kinds of materials they will draw upon. Along the back wall are several filing cabinets which house official documents: the articles of incorporation, deeds to property, the congregation's constitition, mortgages, etc. These are important indicators of the initial purposes, circumstances, and people who brought the church into existence. Also in these cabinets one will find photo files containing "representational sources" from many phases of the congregation's life, and miscellaneous documents which are carefully labelled.

Moving clockwise one finds several shelves holding architects drawings, extra copies of fund-raising brochures and anniversary booklets. (First Church has had several major anniversary celebrations. On each occasion the congregation had the foresight to provide later historians with important resources by publishing an anniversary memento or

Stained glass window of Frances Willard.

booklet.) Then we come to the bound volumes of congregational records which include official pastoral acts (baptisms, weddings, or burials), financial records such as annual budgets and records of contributions, minutes of the official board which was the congregation's central decision-making body, along with minutes and records of many of the more than eighty organizations which have come into being during the congregation's life. These are the places where family influences, economic indicators, and key moments of truth await the historian with the discerning eye. Someone who has wondered about the role of an "elite" family in a church can trace the extent of their power and status here. They can also identify rivalries and factions by close reading of these documents.

Also present on these shelves are copies of the official reports which First Church submitted to its parent Methodist denomination with its statistical summaries of various aspects of congregational life. These are key places for identifying patterns of growth and organization, important decisions in the life of the congregation, and people who played key roles in the church's life.

Part of the distinctive style of this congregation is its propensity for publishing. In 1924, the glossy monthly *The First Church Review* appeared. Two years later the monthly became a four-page weekly. Forty years later the *Review* changed its name to *Soundings*. Beginning with the charter issue a copy of each *Review* has been set aside for the archives — providing a rich cache of data about congregational life. Each organization was encouraged to submit press releases to the staff of First Church's newspaper/magazine, so issues are thick with information about organizational life in the congregation. So serious was First Church about reporting its activities to its members that each organization was required to have a press chairman who prepared news releases according to guidelines set forth in a special manual. (While many congregations do not publish on this scale, most have newsletters or some other pastoral letter which can be plundered for similar insights into congregational life.)

One other special resource this congregation provides for the historian is *The First Church Pulpit*, a published sermon series. The sermons printed here span several decades and offer a special avenue into ministerial perceptions of congregational, denominational, urban, and national life. Careful reading of these documents can provide insights into the major social and theological issues which confronted both pastor and congregation. By paying attention to which topics are mentioned and by noting those that are not, historians can sometimes spot problems in congregational life which never are mentioned in more official or intentional sources like board minutes.

Two of First Church's most prominent preachers were also well-published authors. Dr. Tittle authored thirteen books, and his successor, Dr. Harold Bosley, produced another sixteen. In addition, Dr. Tittle became the subject of an extensive biography which examines the life of this important pastor in the context of the congregation's experience. These books, along with the pastors' personal papers, provide unusual access to the theological and ministerial perspectives of the clergy who served this congregation.

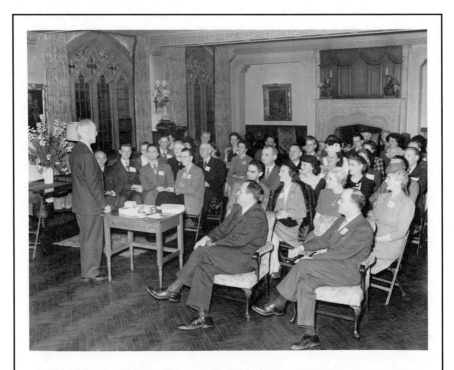

Archives often contain contradictory evidence. This picture of Dr. Tittle teaching suggests harmony and unquestioned authority. However, a resolution from the minutes of the governing board of the congregation (March 6, 1933) shows another side of his tenure.

While most congregations will not have such prolific or celebrated clergy, the personal papers of pastors are precious resources for understanding the rabbi or priest's perspective. They often provide surprising clues to the types of pastoral problems which trouble a congregation and to the major issues which can threaten its unity. In some cases a pastor like Tittle will leave his papers directly in the keeping of a congregation. In other cases, a pastor like Bosley will keep papers in the possession of his or her family, or bequeath them to a seminary or denominational archives. In either case, congregational historians will want to spend a good deal of time exploring these special, if biased, resources.

Further down the shelves in First Church's archives are complete collections of all the worship bulletins used by the congregation. These

---

"For some time a campaign of insinuation, misrepresentation, and slander, much of it anonymous, has been directed against our pastor, Dr. Ernest F. Tittle. We believe that we owe it to him and to our church and to this community to assert unmistakably our loyalty to him and our protest against un-American and unchristian (sic) procedure.

After fourteen years of intimate association with Dr. Tittle as our minister, we would express our absolute confidence in his Christian character and his deep and unselfish devotion to his country, to the church, and to humanity. He is unalterably opposed to the methods of violence advocated by communism, and steadfastly committed to the orderly processes of democratic government.

We stand for a free pulpit and a free church. We do not expect or desire a minister simply to echo the opinions of the congregation, and we do not assert our individual agreement with all of our minister's utterances. But we vigorously resent the effort of outside organizations to dictate to the church or to prescribe its message.

We hold it particularly important in this day that the church should stand apart from all appeals to passion, prejudice, and partisanship, and that our nation should have in the Christian Church a clear, strong voice rising above all divisions, speaking in the name of God for justice, mutual understanding, and good will."

A document like this indicates that something was going on in the congregation's life that so challenged its fundamental values as to evoke a response this strong. The historian will read between the lines and look for additional evidence to fill in what the document leaves out.

can often contain important statistical information — about worship attendance, giving patterns, and the like. But they also provide invaluable glimpses of the shape and character of a congregation's worship life. Styles of liturgical worship, hymn preferences, sermon topics and texts can all be useful clues.

Of special interest to bulletin readers are shifts in worship practice. First Church, for example, had to break with its Methodist tradition when it hosted the World Council of Churches meeting. For the first time since Prohibition it used wine at the sacrament of Holy Communion. In addition the congregation dropped the use of creeds during Pastor Tittle's tenure, and restored them during Pastor Bosley's, an indication of changing stances towards traditional formulations of belief. These "little" omissions or additions can often be the only indicators available to later generations of significant shifts in congregational beliefs and practices.

So far no mention has been made of "immaterial sources," the more illusive of the four categories mentioned by Professors Kyvig and Marty. On the shelves of its archives, First Church possesses tape recordings of a number of interviews with key church members and leaders. This "oral history" is a very important repository for information about customs, traditions, institutions, and the like which may never appear in intentional sources like board minutes. Yet, the character or genius of the congregation, the kind of distinctive quality which was the focus of the first chapter, may be much more accessible through these sources than more conventional written ones.

As I contemplated the treasures awaiting the fortunate historian who could listen to these tapes the archivist reminded me of one more source — the ninety-five people who have belonged to First Church for fifty years or more and who need only to be asked the right questions to open up new facets of the congregation's story. Almost every congregation has its elder men and women, the patriarchs and matriarchs who carry the congregation's memories in their own. With a tape recorder, or increasingly nowadays with a video recorder, the congregational historian has the opportunity to save these important recollections — and those of newer members who may have different perspectives — for future use. Information about how to "do" oral history can be found in the notes at the end of this chapter.

Before closing the door on First Church's archives two additional sources should be mentioned. First is the congregational historian. In this case, Mrs. Katherine Art proved to be a very important resource about the contents of the various sources preserved by the congregation. She knew where to turn for certain types of information and was a ready source of "lore" about the church she served. While not every church will have an archivist like Mrs. Art, perhaps almost every one should have — either salaried or volunteer. But even in the absence of such a resource almost any collection of sources is put together by someone — a pastor, church secretary, or faithful member. That collector may well turn out to be as important a source as the documents he or she has saved.

The second source to be noted as we leave First Church behind is Eleanor Darnall Wallace's *For All The Saints*, the most recent of several histories of the congregation. Again, readers of this volume may not have the advantage of a predecessor who blazed the trail before them. Trailblazers, it must be admitted, do make it easier for those who come after them. But they also can take people down paths which keep very important and beautiful sights out of view. Thus an earlier version of a congregational history can be a rich resource, provided that it is used with caution. Every so often the person seeking to write a fresh history of a congregation will need to step off his predecessor's path in order to fill in aspects of the portrait which were hastily sketched over or inadvertently left out.

With respect to Wallace's book about First Church, then, its importance lies not so much in what it reports as in the questions that lie between its lines. (Such questions can also be found in pastors' sermons, in anniversary booklets, and in official denominational reports.) For example, Mrs. Wallace mentions that Dr. Martin Luther King came to preach at First Church during one of his Chicago visits. She also mentions the pacifist stance of several of the congregation's ministers, the leadership role played by congregation members in the settlement house movement of the early twentieth century, the change of pronouns from *Thou* to *You* in the church's liturgy, and a vote in the early 1970s to change the congregational leadership. But she leaves to the reader's imagination the debates, motives, and understandings which surrounded these pivotal moments in her church's life.

Moments like these — and there were others such as the first ordination of a woman minister, or the earlier decision in the 1930s to sanction dancing and card playing at the church — often get little mention in histories written when memories are fresh and wounds are open. Yet they can be critical incidents in the life of a congregation, indicators of major shifts in belief that have taken place or that are about to occur. Previous versions of a congregation's history thus may mention in a throwaway line or two a turning point which can open up a congregation's history in important and fascinating ways. Where they exist they can be extra resources for the congregational historian. Where they are absent, the congregational historian must pay attention to the unwritten but routinely repeated versions of "official history" which congregation members may be invoking as they explain their traditions to each other. In each case, there are clues to be ferreted out and examined for the historian with the right set of questions.

An overview of a congregation like Evanston's First Church can have the undesired side effect of discouraging historians whose congregations seem to pale in comparison to such powerhouses. Why write a history when there are no clergy superstars, no events of worldwide significance, no members who take their places on lists of movers and shakers?

Part of the answer to such a question comes from the distinctiveness of each place of worship. Different people, traditions, contexts, and experiences come together in each American congregation. Telling the story of even the most plain-looking congregation adds to the richness of our overall portrait of American life. Something precious is lost if only the First Church stories are told.

But another part of the answer appears when we take a second look at what is too easily dismissed as "ordinary." Several of the congregations referred to in this book *could* have been dismissed as ordinary. Zion and St. Margaret's, for example, are congregations with diminished or dwindling resources. Yet they have important stories to tell about human quests for meaning, about love of the neighbor, and about grace under pressure. In the next chapter a rural church that is in many ways the opposite of First Church, Evanston — one with no archives and no immediate claim to fame — is introduced. All three of these places of worship might have been overlooked, except for the fact that one or two gifted observers saw the extraordinariness of these seemingly ordinary places. By giving careful, imaginative attention to these kinds of congregations historians may uncover dimensions of extraordinariness that can surprise even the most jaded observer.

Evanston's First Church then has been described not to demoralize those whose congregations are smaller, plainer, or poorer. On the contrary, it serves as an example of distinctiveness, a reminder of the historian's responsibility to bring into view the hidden or latent specialness present in each congregation.

The Sad Truth

Before this chapter ends it is important to acknowledge a state of affairs that will confront many who use this book. Throughout our nation's history observers from other cultures have helped Americans see the temporal nearsightedness we have as a people. These visitors have pointed out how riveted our attention is to the new and how little room there is for the past in our consciousness. Are they right? All too often the answer seems to be yes. Few of us can recount the names of our great grandparents or great-great grandparents without difficulty, quite unlike people in other cultures who can rattle off genealogies of amazing length with ease. A building that has been around for more than forty years often seems old to us and we have little trouble rationalizing the swing of a wrecker's ball through the remains of a turn-of-the-century building in order to make way for the latest "postmodern" corporate cathedral. For us "the past" may range back a generation or two; on special occasions — the centennial of a church or the bicentennial of the U. S. Constitution — we stretch our memories to include a century or two.

Largely because of our historical amnesia and fundamental orientation to the future, we have often been irresponsible about preserving the very sources that could liberate us from the tyranny of the present moment. More than one congregational historian has told (and — sad to say — more will tell) a horror story about opening a waterlogged box in a forgotten corner of a church basement only to watch irreplaceable original records disintegrate the moment they were touched! Or we continue to hear the one about the too efficient custodian who discarded that box of Pastor So-and-so's sermons because he had been dead for fifty years and room was needed for the church's new xerox machine!

Thus many congregational historians will meet an initial stumbling block — the lack of sources or a very fragmentary collection due to carelessness on the part of previous generations. Such a discouraging discovery need not defeat pursuers of a heritage, however. As this chapter demonstrates, a variety of sources can provide the building blocks for a congregational history. The discovery of knowledge gaps and missing data is part of any historian's job. But part of the historian's craft is learning to identify other sources when a dead end looms at the end of a particular road. And finally, it must be acknowledged that historians frequently have to speculate, to take a "best guess" on the basis of what they have learned elsewhere in their research. The best historians are those who know when they are speculating and when they are standing on more solid ground. They testify to their self-confidence by making clear to their readers when they are shifting from one enterprise to the other.

Some readers will have exactly the opposite problem. Rather than coming up emptyhanded when they begin to look for the important primary sources which historians relish, they find to their dismay that the mounds of data resemble Mt. Everest in size and the Amazon jungle in confusion. There is so much to consider and so many directions that could be taken that the temptation to abort the expedition becomes appealing. Here too, there is reason to continue. Since some sources carry more weight than others, identifying the primary ones can help in mapping a research strategy.

Before plunging in it makes sense to do a preliminary survey of the kinds of materials at hand. Once those have been classified, a plan of action can be designed. Often congregations have a cluster of individuals who are interested in their parish or synagogue's history. When confronted with an overwhelming amount of data it makes sense to form a congregational history committee which can spread the load around and keep morale high as the sifting of data proceeds.

One other preliminary matter merits mention here. Although historians by definition are interested in the past, most of them undertake their efforts in the hope that what they learn and write will make a difference in the present and the future. Many congregations will welcome such a forward-looking concern. One way that such a concern for the future can be expressed is for congregational historians to become protectors of the sources they discover and use. Rather than repeat the mistakes of preceding generations by returning records to unmarked boxes, people who write congregational history need to become zealous defenders and preservers of the sources that future generations will need to write new histories. This book does not offer step by step instructions for setting up congregational archives. But it would fall short of its overall responsibility if it did not urge historians to care about more than their own endeavors. Fire proof boxes, acid-free envelopes, filing systems, and handbooks may be kept on hand to assist congregations in the important task of preserving their past in order that it may live again in future generations. The notes at the end of this chapter suggest some resources to assist with this process.

For Further Reading

David E. Kyvig and Myron A. Marty offer many valuable suggestions to congregational historians in *Nearby History: Exploring the Past Around You* (Nashville: American Association for State and Local History, 1982). The discussion of types of sources occurs on pp. 47-53. Their chapter "Oral Documents" provides an excellent practical introduction to the subject of oral history.

Most denominations have professional archivists who can provide consulting help for congregations that wish to establish archives. Some publish booklets of advice. A letter to the appropriate denominational office from the list in Appendix B may be the shortest route to help. One good example is August Suelflow's *Religious Archives:. An Introduction* (Society of American Archivists Basic Manual Series, Society of American Archivists, 600 S. Federal, Suite 504, Chicago, IL 60605).

·5·

Drawing a Blueprint

A POWERFUL TEMPTATION FACED BY VIRTUALLY ALL historians is the almost irresistible urge to keep piling up data. There is always one more source to check, one more sparkling stone to turn. For congregational historians this means that there will always be one more sermon to read, one more parishioner to interview, one more community newspaper to page through. Granted that historians have an obligation to examine every available piece of important evidence, the simple piling up of facts does not discharge the historical task.

Lest I be misunderstood, I want to express unflinching commitment to the ideal of thorough and systematic research. The narrative the historian writes will be only as good as the raw materials assembled. So careful notetaking systems, attribution of sources, and countless hours of hard work are all assumed. At the same time, however, a hodgepodge of materials, even if every single item glistens like the most expensive imported marble and the pile itself is momentous in its proportions, will be useless unless someone brings a blueprint or plan which can shape these materials into a coherent structure.

This chapter discusses the "blueprint" problem which faces anyone who hopes to interpret a portion of the human past. Although one of the shortest in this book, it may speak very well to the "make or break" factor for every congregational historian.

Creating a Plan

When do you design the plan for a congregational history? Although it may sound premature, I am going to suggest that a first sketch of a blueprint be drawn immediately following the decision to pursue a congregation's history. Such a suggestion immediately evokes cautionary responses. How can someone design a plan without knowing what kinds of materials exist for the project? Won't a plan drawn at this early moment prejudice every subsequent decision about what gets included and what gets left out of the final version? How can a historian possibly distinguish between what is important and what is trivial at this preliminary stage? Won't such an effort be essentially a waste of time since subsequent research will probably require scrapping the original plan and designing a new one?

Objections like these should not be dismissed out of hand. It is true that an early blueprint will need revising as research turns up different kinds of material. It is also true that early hunches can bias every subsequent stage of the effort. Further, somewhere in the midst of the process of historical probing a surprise usually lurks which can necessitate extensive revision of the original plan. Occasionally, treasures of this sort can be so well concealed or so difficult to reconcile with a pre-existing plan that the historian fails to sense their significance and builds without them. Clearly, slavish adherence to early plans is risky.

But so is proceeding without one. To shift metaphors momentarily, if a historian ventures into archives or libraries without some sort of map or plan it is easy to become lost. Without a precise destination in mind it is impossible to tell whether a particular road is a mainstreet to be taken or a detour which eventually leads to a dead end. So there is need for a map or plan to guide the researcher through the maze.

In addition, proceeding without a plan can deceive the researcher about preconceptions. The choice for a congregational historian is not between no plan and a prematurely drawn one. Instead, it is between a conscious or an unconscious one. Drawing the first blueprint at an early stage of inquiry allows many of the taken-for-granted assumptions about this or that place of worship to come into view.

Do I believe this congregation is God's chosen vehicle for ministry to a particular group of people? Or do I regard it as a place for members of the status conscious middle class to escape from the realities of everyday existence? Has it made mistakes in its social stances or scriptural interpretations? Have its clergy been saints or rascals? Have its people been active ministers of God with wills of their own or weather vanes subject to whichever clerical breeze happens to have been blowing?

Such usually hidden assumptions, and many more alluded to in chapter 1, determine research strategies and final outcomes. My point here is: sketching one's plan at the outset offers two advantages. It allows for an organized approach to the effort. And it forces the author to become conscious of his or her assumptions.

There is an important corollary to my "plan early" priniciple, however. To choose to draw a careful blueprint at the outset requires an accompanying willingness to participate in an ongoing process of proposing "Plan Bs." As research proceeds, the old "Plan A" inevitably becomes obsolete, sometimes in part, often in toto. But rather than regarding such reciprocity between planning the project and carrying it out as a time-wasting liability, I view the interactive process as an asset. In essence, a process of refinement takes place which parallels that of building design. First, rough sketches are drawn. Then, more careful architectural renderings appear. Finally, a mature blueprint is prepared — subject, of course, to changes necessitated in the actual construction process. Regular interaction between blueprint drawing and consideration of materials allows one simultaneously to pursue a specific line of inquiry and be open to new discoveries.

The Elements of a Historical Blueprint

If a historical blueprint is going to result in a functional and aesthetically pleasing edifice, certain basic rules of thumb need to be kept in mind. Just as architects must pay attention to the workings of gravity, the tolerance of materials, the resources and aspirations of clients, the "fit" between structure and environment, and latest developments in the state of their art as they prepare their drawings, so historians work with basic considerations as they make their plans.

If gravity provides the architect with her fundamental point of departure, then chronology plays a similar role for the historian. Ignore gravity and any architectural vision will collapse into rubble. Ignore chronology and the result will be a historical shambles. Historians must ascertain when actual events occurred. Their first attempt at ordering data is to place them temporally, to put first things first, second things second, and so on.

As historians arrange their discoveries chronologically — whether those be from first impressions, consideration of landscape features, or archival plunderings — they look for connections. Did this influx of a new ethnic group in the 1950s contribute to the decision to add an additional worship service in the 1960s? Did a denominational decision in the 1970s to ordain women into ministry provide a stimulus for this congregation's recent controversy over the role of women in its life? Was Mrs. Smith's experience with the charismatic movement in the 1960s the first stirring of spiritual revival which crested in her church's turn to home Bible study programs in the 1980s? Only the patient arrangement of data along a timeline can make it possible to identify such questions and then pursue them. Chronology becomes the backbone, or to return to the architectural metaphor, the plumbline, of any historical blueprint.

Once the chronology has been established — and this is not as easy as it sounds since human memories and records are often mistaken — then it becomes possible to look for two major types of phenomena. The most apparent are the turning points or decisive shifts in a congregation's life. Fire in the sanctuary or the dedication of a new building, defrocking a pastor or calling a new one, collapse of a community's economy or the surprise bequest from a wealthy member's estate — these are events which make indelible marks upon a community of faith. Often a congregation's character can be given decisive shape in a moment of crisis and that shape may endure for generations. Such critical incidents often clarify character as they manifest central values and conflicts. So the historian scans a congregation's timeline looking for the jagged interruptions.

But turning points can also be deceptive. Because they are frequently easy to spot and often sit firmly in the memories of congregation members, they can obscure other important dynamics and developments. For that reason, it is important to probe chronologically arranged material for a second type of change: the gradual shifts and developments which, though lacking in drama and visibility, often have very strong effects.

Was this parish undergoing a gradual professionalization of its membership during the middle years of the twentieth century? Does the fact that its membership gradually moved from blue-collar jobs to university-trained careers tell us more about the shifting relations between priests and people than the usual explanation which invokes the fresh theological formulations of the Second Vatican Council as the decisive factor? Or, in another congregation, was the quiet democratization of biblical studies with its accompanying gradual infusion of alternative perspectives more responsible for a decision to call a female pastor than a sudden denominational decision to certify women for ministry?

What is suggested here as a second element in constructing a blueprint is a careful searching of a congregation's chronology for both dramatic turning points and quiet developments. Once both types of phenomena are in view it becomes possible to propose a new Plan B for organizing further work. Will this turning point become the focal point for the entire congregational plot? Or will a dominant trend or dynamic become the main theme for the history about to be written? The answer can only come after both types of change have been identified and appraised. And the historian needs to keep in mind that most congregations cannot be adequately understood without an integrative interpretation which relates both gradual and sudden forms of historical development. And, of course, the non-event of sameness should not be overlooked either.

As one ponders the material found along the timeline it is essential that a bifocal perspective be maintained. On the one hand it is important that the historian be a critical observer who examines every assumption and explanation about why events happened the way they did. But on the other it is equally important to enter imaginatively into the congregation's experience, searching for access to its vantage point at decisive moments and in everyday life. Here the lessons learned from participant observation can help. But historians go on to ask: How did these people understand the crisis before them, the conflict that divided them, or the behavior that seemed so normal to them? As the historian migrates between insider and outsider perspectives it becomes possible to fill in components of the blueprint with materials that are both accurate and fair to the people who actually experienced such events.

The Example of Meridian, Idaho

One way to demonstrate the importance of blueprints is to examine a sample congregational history. For our purposes a recently completed history of First United Methodist Church of Meridian, Idaho, serves as a useful case in point. Written in 1986, *They Came To Build A Community* tells the one-hundred-year story of a congregation begun during the years when the last parcels of the American frontier were settled. Unlike

Evanston's First Methodist Church discussed in the previous chapter, this congregation did not come to life and flourish in an environment shaped by the suburban development of one of this nation's major cities. Instead, the people who lived in this small town (Meridian's population didn't top fifteen hundred until 1946) faced a hard, rural life, which in its early years revolved almost exclusively around the daily chores of homesteading.

Here we do not find stories of the upward mobility of corporate executives, university professors, and other professionals who could count on Chicago for their daily needs. Rather, we read about people whose early years were spent in hand-to-hand combat with an inhospitable environment. Their concerns were daily battles against sage brush, seasonal skirmishes with waves of rabbits and locusts which threatened whatever crops could be coaxed from the dry land, and, above all else, the search for a reliable source of water which could make possible the rest of their dreams.

New York Canal (near Boise, Idaho).

They Came To Build A Community merits attention for several reasons. First, its authors, Lila Hill and Glen W. Davidson, have provided access to a way of life which could easily slip into oblivion as our nation goes on its modernizing way. Photographs of the digging of "the Ditch" (the

Pioneer Lady and First Home on the Desert (near Boise, Idaho).

irrigation canal which transformed a barren landscape with its "one lone tree" into productive farm land), or of the simple shelters occupied by the first settlers evoke the feel of an era which seems almost as remote to most late twentieth-century people as the ages of dinosaurs and ice.

In quiet but persuasive ways the photos, maps, and graphs which accompany the text of this congregational history remind readers of the signficance of long forgotten institutions and individuals. The creamery which for decades gave Meridian its major source of income, the circuit-riding preacher who first brought the Methodist gospel to Idaho, the packing boxes of a once prosperous but now defunct dried fruit industry — these images transport readers into a world very different from their own. The distance between then and now becomes more apparent when our eyes scan a table of price comparisons between 1897 and 1986. At the turn of the century a farmer could purchase his basic farm equipment — one horse and plow — for $10. Now Meridian's farmers must spend more than $135,000 for the basics — an eighty-horse-power tractor, plow, disc, baler, swather, and baled-hay hauler.

The particularity of this rural western world with its distinctive ethos, terrain, and experiences comes into view through the window of one

Meridian, Idaho, c. 1910.

small congregation. The view of Meridian seen here casts other types of congregational experience into sharper relief. It is quite distinct from the black Pentecostal church in Pittsburgh or the Methodist church in Evanston. Such an encounter helps historians of very different types of congregations become more aware of the distinctiveness of the particular place of worship which occupies their energies.

But the book about the Idaho church has more to teach us. The title selected by the authors announces their choice of a central theme for their congregation's history. These historians decided that the basic human endeavor of building a community was the resilient thread which could weave together the various strands of their story. From the moment the first settlers stepped off the Oregon Trail in the 1880s up to First United's decision in 1978 to print a pictorial directory of its membership, one dynamic seems to recur. The people who tamed this piece of earth struggled for more than mere existence. As the congregation's pastor said in the book's foreword, *"They Came To Build A Community* is the history of a people from various backgrounds with differences of social and economic status and of competing political views who, nevertheless, were forged together by the intention of creating a community in an arid land."

Three architectural moments in a congregation's story. Clockwise from upper left: Methodist Episcopal Church, South (1895); Methodist Episcopal Church (1908); First United Methodist Church (1978).

That basic drive towards community endured long beyond the time when water was so scarce that people fought and killed for it. Although the congregation now has a modern church building with all the accouterments of most suburban congregations — offering envelopes, worship bulletins, choir robes, an organ, two Sunday morning services, a church secretary — its basic quest for a community of people who shared a common Methodist vision continues, although in a different form from the church's early days.

Once the authors decided upon the main line of their story it became possible to develop a structure. The first half of the book gives attention to developments within the village of Meridian itself. The internal life of the congregation became the focus of the second half of the book. Throughout both halves "community" served as the thematic line upon which the authors could hang all of the information gleaned from their research. So information about the first settlers, the way the land was promoted to attract them, the new technologies which advanced agricultural possibilities, the economic depressions, and the various local institutions such as the Grange, the 4-H Club, and other fraternal organizations all found places in the first half of their book.

In the second half readers are introduced to the people and pastors who worked so hard to make their church a community of faith which could support this rural life. Unlike Evanston's First Church, this congregation had few long pastorates and no superstar clergy. Yet the institutional milestones of each pastorate — parish revivals, the decisions to build new parsonages, the creation of new women's and youth organizations, the arrival of the telephone, and the advent of the first electric stove — all find their places in this internal part of the church's story.

This church also had its traumatic moments, its turning points. In its precarious early days the fledgling congregation dismissed and then defrocked its founding pastor, J.D. Flenner, after charges about financial irregularities were brought against him. Five years later it divided into two congregations along lines left over from the Civil War. Another twenty-three years passed before the two congregations buried their hatchets and reunited. But for a variety of reasons the authors chose the ongoing search for community over such crisis points as the key to their project's organization.

The choice of "community" for this congregation's theme was

especially apt. During early years of settlement the Methodist congregation was the only church in the area. Its being first on the scene made possible an overlap situation which allowed the congregation to play a shaping role in the larger community. Since there were few institutions of any sort during Meridian's formative years, the church often fulfilled many "community" functions which took place beyond the walls of their church buildings. Even when new religious groups sought to create their own congregations, First Church frequently served as host and enabler. The congregation kept the threshold between itself and the town quite low — so that community issues inevitably became church matters. Thus during temperance days the congregation played a key role in establishing the larger community's character. Meridian became the first Idaho town to ratify Prohibition and prior to that decision had been noteworthy for its lack of saloons. Those stances were shaped in large part by the town's Methodists, the members of First United Church.

But concern for community also was close to the heart of the Methodist tradition which these people cherished. For them, building a decent, pleasant community was an expression of God's creating activity. Care for their neighbors was a way of responding to God's presence in their midst. So "community" pointed to more than the context for their church's story. It also identified the distinctive concerns and beliefs which gave the congregation its reason for being.

Before turning from First Methodist's story to the larger religious, social, and cultural plots which surround local congregations (the subject of chapter 6) it is important to note two things. First, the congregational history written about this church was shaped in very important ways by the type of resources available — or unavailable — to these historians. In 1923 a major fire destroyed much of downtown Meridian — along with many key records which are lost forever. No treasure trove of information securely hidden in a church archives was waiting for the inquiring historian to plunder. So these authors had to turn to community newspapers and family histories for much of their data. Perhaps if there had been more information about the day-to-day life of the church — its organizations, its pastors, etc., a different kind of history would have been written. But — and this is the second point — notice how much can be learned about a congregation even when the more conventional types of data are not available!

Clearly raw materials shape the final product. But it is also true that the history of a congregation only comes into view when such material is shaped by a vision or blueprint. Further refining of that vision is the subject of the next chapter.

For Further Reading

Lila Hill and Glen W. Davidson, *They Came to Build a Community: A History of Meridian, Idaho, and the People Called Methodists* (Meridian, Idaho: First United Methodist Church, 1986).

·6·

Weaving Plots Together

IN 1967 BRITISH PLAYWRIGHT TOM STOPPARD TURNED the tables on the Shakespearean tradition with his play, *Rosencrantz & Guildenstern Are Dead*. Stoppard did so by making two lesser known characters from *Hamlet* the stars of his drama. While Rosencrantz and Guildenstern dominate center stage, Hamlet, Claudius, Ophelia, and Gertrude spend most of their time waiting in the wings, quite a reversal for some of the "juiciest" roles in English theatre.

Most readers will recall that Shakespeare's classic drama revolves around some of the grand plots in human experience: revenge for the death of a father; ambivalence in the face of duty; ambition of the highest order; and struggles with questions about the meaning and purpose of life. Kings, princes, and powerful people stride across the Shakespearean stage, occasionally pausing to interact with their inferiors. Although Rosencrantz and Guildenstern appear frequently, they are clearly of little interest to Shakespeare except as people who do the bidding of kings and princes. Like pawns in someone else's chess game, they carry messages, run errands, and try to ingratiate themselves with the powers that be. At no time does Shakespeare show interest in these characters for their own sake. They remain one-dimensional, easily forgettable, "bit" parts in a tiny subplot.

Stoppard on the other hand makes their thoughts and perspectives the central motif of his play. If an audience did not already know the plot line of "the Hamlet" they could leave Stoppard's play with little awareness of Hamlet's "madness," Ophelia's grief, or Claudius' perfidy. Hamlet's eloquent questions about the meaning of life go unasked. Instead, Stoppard focuses attention on what it means to be a pawn in someone else's game. What this modern playwright helps us see is that there is more to the tale of Hamlet than even an artist as great as Shakespeare could disclose. There is more drama in life than that disclosed in the tragic encounters of kings and princes. There are other perspectives, other stories, other plots.

What do Shakespeare and Stoppard have to do with writing congregational history? Few of us can create a drama, or coax words into quotable lines the way these two authors have. But each congregational historian is faced with a version of their formidable challenge. They must address the "which plot" problem. In essence, the congregational historian's tasks are to ferret out all the plot lines contained within the life of a particular congregation, to select the important ones, and then to connect these filaments of story with those that stretch beyond it into familial, denominational, social, and religious histories. Answers to the "which plot" question should incorporate elements which would be of interest to both Shakespeare and Stoppard. To see how that is done we again turn to a congregation, this time Temple Israel of Boston. At the conclusion of this overview I will list the plots which intersect in this one congregation's history. Perhaps as a way of sharpening their own plot-detecting skills readers will want to keep a mental list to compare with mine.

One Temple, Many Plots

Just a quick scan of the table of contents for *Growth and Achievement: Temple Israel 1854-1954* indicates that this book's authors recognized several distinct plots in the history of their place of worship. Words like American Jewry, Boston, and congregational life in the first three chapter titles point to three of the most important. Later chapters feature several of Temple Israel's distinguished rabbis, each of whom left a lasting mark on the congregation. Altogether the eight chapters suggest that at least that many plots run through the story this book seeks to tell. Are there more?

In 1854, twenty-five members of Boston's first Jewish temple, Ohabei Shalom, created a new congregation, Adath Israel. Notwithstanding Ohabei Shalom's fine new building and many resources, this predominantly German group of Jews had reached an impasse with a Polish faction in their temple. Although the leaders of this splinter group intended to create a more congenial version of the Orthodox *shul* they had left behind in Germany, they had also set out on a path which later became known as the reform movement in Judaism.

Sources are spotty for these early years, but we do get glimpses of a synagogue making careful and frugal plans for its worship life. In 1862 their treasury dwindled to $5.62 while Rabbi Shoniger's salary climbed from $200.00 to $450.00. Their first synagogue building had room for two hundred people, with women carefully segregated to a gallery above the men. When President Lincoln was assassinated in 1865, Adath Israel's members expressed their Americanness with special services advertised in the Boston *Herald*. The synagogue, an American flag, and a portrait of the slain president were draped with $13.75 worth of black cotton to express their sorrow.

Less than a decade later the synagogue took a major step down the road of reform by selecting Solomon Schindler as its new rabbi. By that time the congregation was prosperous enough to offer a $1500.00 salary and to advertise for candidates. Schindler responded to their ad and began a twenty-year association which would lead Adath Israel through an identity transition that left the congregation looking more like an American church with a pastor than a conventional Jewish synagogue.

With Schindler's encouragement, women came down from the gallery and joined the men on the main floor. An organ, choir, and new prayer book transformed worship life from its distinctive Jewish pattern to a much more American one. These shifts may not seem all that dramatic to readers of Protestant backgrounds, but to Jews who possessed no traditions of organs, choirs, and the like these changes were drastic enough to lead to fifteen resignations from the roster of forty.

Still, Schindler did not hesitate on his march towards reform. He led the congregation from its home in downtown Boston to a new Romanesque building in the city's fashionable South End. No sooner had the congregation moved into its new home than he introduced Sunday services, a marked departure from the centuries of Sabbath observance so central to Judaism.

Yet while Schindler's innovations drove some away, they appealed to others. By the time Schindler had moved his congregation to the South End, one hundred of Boston's most influential Jews were on Temple Israel's membership rolls. Moreover, Schindler's success did not end at the borders of Boston's Jewish community. At the dedication of their new Temple three of the leading lights of American Protestantism, the reverends Minot J. Savage, Edward Everett Hale, and Phillips Brooks, gave addresses. The congregation's historians report that on some Sundays there were as many non-Jews as Jews listening to Schindler's sermons. These messages — so out of character in form and content with classic Judaism — were of such public appeal that they were reprinted in the The Globe, one of Boston's leading newspapers.

While the main import of Schindler's program was devoted to making the "Jew like the Gentile" in ceremonial matters, Schindler was also intent upon transforming the beliefs of his congregants. He welcomed insights from biblical criticism, comparative religion, and evolutionary theory. Rejecting the idea of an intimately involved personal God and abandoning expectations of a coming Messiah, Schindler accommo-dated himself to the dominant mood of his day as he substituted belief in human progress for some of the central tenets of traditional Jewish belief.

Eventually his "religion of humanity" carried him beyond the pale of even the most reformed strands of Judaism. For a time Edward Bellamy's religion of social reform and some of the ideas of other "Free Religion-ists" then circulating in cosmopolitan Boston seemed more congenial. By the time he stepped down as rabbi in 1893, Schindler had challenged most of Judaism's cherished traditions. A rabbi who felt Jews could learn much from Jesus, who advocated intermarriage, and who admitted that he was a socialist and an agnostic, had led his congregation quite far on the journey toward reform before they parted ways.

What about the people who called Schindler to his rabbinate and who supported him? What do we know about them? Historian Arthur Mann felt that "it is doubtful that Solomon Schindler's aspirations were ever identical to those of his congregants. The latter wished to retain their Jewish identity, Schindler wanted to destroy it." Yet while their rabbi went too far too fast, Schindler's efforts to adjust his faith to its American context were exactly what his people wanted. Temple Israel was a congregation made up of people who sought to adapt to the American way of life. These were people who had "made it"; they wanted to fit religiously as well as socially and economically.

The selection of Charles Fleischer as Schindler's successor in 1894 indicates that while Schindler may have outdistanced his constituency, Temple Israel nonetheless wanted to continue on reform's path. Fleischer succeeded in permanently establishing Sunday services in 1907, accomplishing what his predecessor had started but failed to establish. He initiated pulpit exchanges with Christian preachers and turned Temple Israel into a civic forum. There he and other champions of causes could advocate equal rights for women, planned parenthood and eugenics while opposing capital punishment and American imperialism against Filipinos.

Like Schindler, Fleischer moved his congregation into a new building, this time one which boldly emphasized its Middle Eastern roots. Yet Fleischer was even more of an Americanist than Schindler. By 1911 he too had moved sufficiently beyond his tradition to result in a second separation of rabbi and congregation. So drawn to the Transcendentalism which flourished in Boston that "he made it known that he preferred Emerson to Moses," Fleischer left Temple Israel; from there he moved on to found the Sunday Commons, a New England-style nonsectarian religion which sought to fuse America's pluralist tribes into a new inclusive church with a democratic faith. Even Schindler's clockmaker God was too confining for Fleischer. Many believed that this rabbi was more of a Pantheist or Transcendentalist than anything else.

Was Fleischer simply pursuing his own vision? Hardly. In 1909 Harvard's President Charles Eliot (who in private correspondence acknowledged his intellectual kinship with Fleischer) also proclaimed the need for a new religion which revered truth, science, the individual, and social service. This cosmopolitan religion, which seemed to flourish among Boston's Unitarians, as well as some of its Jews and academics, counted followers in many places where elites struggled to reconcile old claims of faith with new forms of knowledge. But it also drew fire from its critics. Ironically, one of those critics was Solomon Schindler. The emeritus rabbi felt constrained to preach one more sermon, which he titled "Mistakes I Have Made." Once the trailblazer of reform Schindler now tried to apply the brakes to what he and Fleischer had set in motion. The attempt to make Jews "like the Gentiles" had gone too far, even for him.

Temple Israel opted neither for Schindler's late-in-life effort at repristination nor Fleischer's cosmopolitan transcendentalism. Instead, they chose a moderate rabbi, Harry Levi, who welcomed reform but refused to let go of his heritage. Levi led Temple Israel to its place as "the foremost synagogue in New England." A gifted administrator and a defender of "the melting pot" image of America, Levi preached sermons on the radio, constructed a meeting house for all the new activities of his congregation, and stressed compatability between Judaism and humanism.

Under his leadership Temple Israel zigzagged between its heritage and modernity. In 1912 Saturday services were initiated. A congregational seder was inaugurated in 1913. But alongside these attempts at retrieval of an ancient heritage came the abolition of assigned pews in 1922 and the election of the first woman to the temple's board of trustees in 1924. Levi also promoted more interfaith activities, a theatre group and a vigorous adult education program — all indicators of the increasing sophistication and Americanness of his congregation. Religious education was so important during this rabbi's tenure that Temple Israel's Sunday School (remember, this was a Protestant invention!) became the first in the nation to pay its teachers.

Toward the end of Levi's rabbinate, events in the United States and around the world began to call into question the accommodation these Jews had achieved with modernity. Economic depression, the rise of Nazism in Germany and anti-Semitism in the United States challenged progressive assumptions which had seemed self-evident to people like Schindler and Fleischer. A new rabbi, Joshua Loth Liebman, took office in 1939 during an era when his constituents began to search for roots and distinctiveness again. Soon Friday evening services returned and Temple Israel "went to synagogue and not to church." Young boys began to celebrate Bar Mitzvah in addition to the much more American event known as confirmation. Jews began to reassert their peoplehood, and Temple Israel abandoned the anti-Zionist posture of earlier Reform Judaism to call for the establishment of a Jewish state of Israel.

Liebman also participated in the spirit of his age by welcoming insights from psychiatry. Not only did he find his own experience of psychoanalysis helpful, he went on to incorporate the insights from this major stream in modern consciousness in a bestseller, *Peace of Mind*, which was translated into fourteen languages and sold more than 700 thousand copies.

Perhaps the best symbol for the Temple's journey is the tallith, the ancient prayer stole which has been worn by pious Jews for millennia. The tallith had almost disappeared at Temple Israel during the days when reform and accommodation were at their zenith. By the 1950s Rabbi Roland Gittelsohn could put his tallith on and edit *The*

Reconstructionist magazine without alienating a synagogue which at an earlier time would have viewed such overt retrievals with some embarrassment. The disappearance and reappearance of that ancient stole attest to the ongoing dialogue between a modern congregation and its ancient heritage — one that takes place in many congregations besides this one.

How Many Plots?

Not every congregation will have professional historians on hand — as Temple Israel did — to guide their history-writing process. So in many ways it seems unfair to hold up this Temple's history as an example. Yet even if we grant that few amateur historians come equipped with a ready-made inventory of historical themes and subplots like the ones Arthur Mann and his colleagues brought to their task, it is also true that they did what all historians can do — they connected an individual reality to its larger context.

For our purposes, Temple Israel is important because it suggests several specific plot lines to watch for. Consideration of this synagogue's multiplottedness can awaken a basic sensitivity which will help the congregational historian speak to a wider audience.

This is not to say that the history of Temple Israel we have just reviewed is the perfect example for all congregational historians to emulate. On the contrary, it seems to lean towards the Shakespearean rather than the Stoppardean mode of storytelling. Yet, in its day (1954), *Growth and Achievement* represented a signficant advance over conventional approaches to American religious history which followed denominational trajectories and concentrated on atypical religious leaders. Very few scholars got as close to congregational reality as these authors did. But there still is a bit of a "kings and princes" feel to this history, with more attention paid to the Schindlers and Fleischers than to the people who played Rosencrantz and Guildenstern parts. So even while learning lessons from this good example, we will want to look for plots that got little attention.

How many plots were there? Lists will vary, but let me suggest at least the following:

A. American Judaism.
B. Boston.
C. New England Transcendentalism.
D. Ohabei Shalom.
E. Solomon Schindler.
F. Feminism.
G. Anti-Semitism.
H. Charles Fleischer.
I. The United States of America.
J. Progressivism.
K. Joshua Loth Liebman.
L. Roland Gittelsohn.
M. The Middle Class.
N. The Sunday School.
O. Planned Parenthood.
P. Harvard University.
Q. The Media.
R. German Immigrants.

This list is not exhaustive. In fact more plot lines emerge in portions of Temple Israel's history which went unmentioned here. But the eighteen listed above suggest the complex web of story lines that permeate a congregational history. Some of these story lines seem to be quite thin. For example, feminism comes into view only through mention of seating-pattern changes and the election of a woman trustee. Yet recent study of feminism and early women's rights movements indicates how large that plot was and how important churches and synagogues were in its development.

Harvard University has an oblique connection — made explicit in the cosmopolitan kinship shared by President Eliot and Rabbi Fleischer — but it presumably also played roles in the lives of various families of the Temple. Planned Parenthood and the Sunday School were minor motifs, but they indicated the way Protestant and secular concerns were welcomed into the Temple's life. Abraham Lincoln's funeral commemoration reminds us of the way national events impinge upon congregational life. But we also need to keep in mind the way a national religious style — complete with organs, sermons, choirs, and full churches on Sundays — seeps into congregational life. And within the plot line of Judaism there are all sorts of subplots which can be glimpsed in this

Temple's story. Most prominent is the story of Reform Judaism, but the ebbs and flows of Zionism, the emergence of a retraditioning movement, and the classic debate over the core character of Judaism can all be seen.

Resources for Dealing with Plot Questions

If your congregation is like most it will have no professional historian to draw upon like those at hand in Temple Israel. And since the skills of the historian have never been the exclusive possession of a professional guild that need not be a cause for despair. In fact when help is needed with the "which plot" problem there are several clear paths to follow.

A. *Consult your local or state historical society.* Most communities have recognized the need to preserve and study their histories. By creating societies which specialize in nearby history, communities make it possible for citizens to discover the social, economic, institutional, educational, political, and familial contexts which give the most immediate shape to a particular congregation's experience. Here are the places (along with the local library) where community newspapers, photo collections, firsthand accounts, and the like may be found to fill in the gaps left by spotty congregational archives. These are natural places to ask questions about community perceptions of a congregation, about the difference made in community life by a given group of people.

B. *Visit denominational archives.* If your particular congregation belongs to or at some point was a member of a larger denomination then many resources may be assembled in such collections. Find out if all resources are held at one national center or if the collection is dispersed along regional or state lines. If the latter is the case, then visits to each may be in order.

The first thing to ask is what special collections of material the archives contain about your individual congregation. Perhaps Pastor Smith's widow sent all her husband's personal papers there when she moved into retirement housing. More likely will be files of official reports submitted by your congregation to its parent denomination. In addition, there will be resources on major denomination-wide events here. If a pastor or rabbi took sides in a controversy over the role of women in the church, liturgical reform, or issues of biblical interpretation, it is likely that a denomination's archives will have primary and secondary sources which can give a more complete picture of such a controversy than that available from the viewpoint of an individual congregation's resources.

This is the place to inquire about written denominational histories, the careers of clergy who served in other places besides your particular church or synagogue, membership statistics, local and churchwide growth and giving patterns, and the like. In recent years many of these centers have made strenuous efforts to collect materials from local congregations. Jewish Theological Seminary in New York City, for example, has developed a special collection for Conservative synagogue materials. So has Hebrew Union College in Cincinnati for Reform Judaism. Many of these archives have published specialized materials for people who want to understand the history of congregations within their particular church body. A listing of various denominational archives is contained in appendix B of this book.

C. *Consult your local church historian.* If one of your denomination's seminaries is not too distant, it makes sense to invite its expert on the denomination's story to lunch. By sharing the central features of your congregation's story and asking for help in identifying connections between it and the stories which are central to the denomination, it may be possible to find places where your congregation enters and exits that larger story. In addition, this historian should be able to point to resources about other denominations that may connect to a particular congregation. This individual may be a good critical reader to share a first draft with — and such sharing may offer the church historian some Stoppardean insights into the denomination's story as well.

If your "own" seminary proves too distant, or if your congregation does not belong to a denomination, it may be possible to consult a local church historian from the religion department of a nearby university or at a seminary of a denomination which has nothing to do with your particular congregation. These scholars can ask questions, point to reference works, and spot connections between parts of an individual congregation's experience and other developments in the American religious context.

D. *Read books that follow some of the major plots that you have identified in your congregation's story.* In order to identify some of the larger plots in the American religious story most historians turn to the scholars who have devoted careers to such inquiry. Two such scholars are Martin E. Marty and Sydney E. Ahlstrom. Marty's recent *Pilgrims in Their Own Land* provides a single volume overview of the five-hundred-year-long plot of American religious life. Here a reader can gain a sense of the tremendous religious vitality and variety which has characterized so much of our nation's life. The interaction of religious and social plots; the ways in which feminism, temperance, civil rights, and benevolent movements crisscrossed denominational lines; the great common experiences of so many American religious groups — the experience of the frontier, the encounter with the city and secularity, the shared heritage of religious freedom and disestablishment fostered by the American Revolution, the dynamism of religious revivalism — these are just some of the subplots Marty identifies and weaves together into one story. *Pilgrims* is not a place to turn for close-up study of one of the many distinct American religious plots, but it is the best place to turn for a single synthetic overview of the entire American religious story.

Another of Marty's books can be useful for those seeking help with plotlines. In *A Nation of Behavers* Marty draws a new behavioral map of American religion which calls attention to six major zones, or behavioral regions. Suggesting that paying attention to whether people (here read congregations) fit into mainline, evangelical-fundamentalist, pentecostal-charismatic, ethnic, new, or civil religious categories may tell us more about them than information as to whether they are Lutheran, Methodist, Catholic, or Jewish. Marty's map calls attention to six additional plot lines which may run through almost any congregation's story.

Sydney Ahlstrom's *A Religious History of the American People* provides a different kind of help. While he also sought to pay attention to the entire American religious story, Ahlstrom's work gave primary attention to its Protestant and Puritan strands. Since those strands have until recently been the predominant ones in the American self-understanding, Ahlstrom's attention to those plot lines makes sense. And his history remains an essential reference for those who seek the relations between that story and their own. Thus, Ahlstrom's discussions of transcendentalism, Unitarianism, and other offshoots of New England Puritanism, would be natural places to turn, if like Temple Israel, a congregation's story included those dimensions.

There are of course enormous literatures about each of the denominations, social movements, cities, political campaigns, etc., that run through our congregational stories. This book cannot begin to list them, but it can urge historians to seek resources on Judaism, Catholicism, abolitionism, progressivism, and the like when they seem appropriate.

Before concluding this chapter, one additional resource should be mentioned. In the last few years several scholars have begun to specialize in congregational history. Jay Dolan, a church historian at Notre Dame University, for example, has published several books about Catholic parishes and recently has developed his own plot line for Catholic parish history. In addition, he has edited a larger work which focuses on parish history within distinct regions of the United States. Jack Wertheimer of Jewish Theological Seminary in New York has edited a volume devoted to synagogue history which deals with specific aspects of that particular variety of congregational history.

These works, along with an enormous uncatalogued literature of local church histories, suggest that there are many models and resources on the scene or coming on to the scene which can assist the individual congregational historian. In addition, a new organization, the American Guild of Religious Historiographers, seeks to meet the needs of congregational historians.

All of these resources can help congregational historians make creative use of the mountains of data they have gathered. While their histories may never find themselves on shelves next to works by Tom Stoppard or William Shakespeare, congregational historians who find the crosswalks between their particular projects and the larger plots of culture, history, religion, denomination, and community will have taken a significant step closer to a larger audience than the membership of their particular church or synagogue.

For Further Reading

Tom Stoppard, *Rosencrantz and Guildenstern are Dead* (New York: Grove Press, Inc., 1967).

Arthur Mann, editor, *Growth and Achievement: Temple Israel, 1854-1954* (Cambridge, Mass.: The Riverside Press, 1954). See especially pp. v, 59, 68, 102.

Martin E. Marty, *Pilgrims in Their Own Land* (Boston: Little, Brown and Company, 1984) and *A Nation of Behavers* (Chicago: The University of Chicago Press, 1976).

Sydney Ahlstrom, *A Religious History of the American People* (New Haven: Yale University Press, 1972).

Jay Dolan, "The American Catholic Parish: A Historical Perspective, 1820-1980," in David Byers, editor, *The Parish in Transition* (Washington, D.C.: United States Catholic Conference, 1986) and Jay Dolan, editor, *The American Catholic Parish: A History from 1850 to the Present* (New York: Paulist Press, 1987).

Jack Wertheimer, editor, *The American Synagogue: A Sanctuary Transformed* (New York: Cambridge University Press, 1987).

Many readers may wish to contact The American Guild of Religious Historiographers (3500 Fuller, NE, Grand Rapids, MI 49505) for help with specific problems encountered in their research.

· 7 ·

Crafting A History

Imagination

HOW DOES A HISTORIAN PROCEED FROM THE CONCERNS
of the preceding chapters — piles of data, timelines, files of thematic
material, and hunches about the plot of a particular congregation — to
the finished product, to the mature narrative history? At the risk of
sounding a bit mystical, I want to begin answering that question by
refering to what a distinguished medievalist once called "the historical
experience." Just as lovers recall their first kiss, touch, or glance, R. W.
Southern remembers the first time he had this much-less-common
experience. Assigned at age fifteen the "depressing" schoolboys' task of
writing an essay on King Henry VII, Southern was glum: "Acres of facts
and intolerable dreariness and frightening unintelligibility stretched out
in all directions numbing the senses." Then something unexpected
happened. "Suddenly, out of nowhere, the precious words formed
themselves in my mind. I can see them yet. They were: Henry VII was
the first King of England who was a business man."

From the vantage point of maturity and accomplishment Southern
readily admits that his interpretation turned out to be "wrong."
Hindsight gained through further study taught him that there were
better — or more adequate — ways to account for Henry's distinctive
kingship than his "business man" hypothesis. But that does not mean
that the entire experience should be discounted.

Even though Southern's boyhood theory resulted in a flawed interpretation, it still instructs. It reveals a fundamental ambiguity in the task
of history writing. On the one side is the exhilaration of discovery. Part
of the sheer joy of historical research is the thrill that accompanies

turning up a previously lost document, a forgotten person, or an unnoticed event. At a less exhilarating level, historical study depends upon the stating of theses in order for research to be purposeful rather than haphazard. So at each step of the process a historian seeks to present the best explanation available so that additional knowledge can be gained.

But there is another side. Sooner or later most historians learn that each flash of insight — no matter how powerful it initially seems — will in the light of someone's hindsight need revising. As they overturn outdated understandings historians set themselves up for a similar fate. Recognition of this ongoing process need not demoralize us, however. Instead a humble awareness of one's debt to past interpreters and enthusiastic welcome of the present situation's new needs and opportunities for fresh thinking can motivate and inspire.

This book is not the place to explore all the dimensions of this ambiguity. Instead its purpose is to invite congregational historians to take the risk of fully entering it. If more is to emerge from all their labors than "acres of facts" or "intolerable dreariness and frightening unintelligibility" then each historian must take the imaginative step of proposing a thesis, or explanation, which best accounts for all the data unearthed and the developments noted. Something akin to Southern's historical experience is needed.

What counts as such an experience? Southern provides three clues: "First, it was very sharp and vivid; second, it had a private and personal significance; and third, it worked." Some may feel that this talk about "the historical experience" sounds much too unscientific, way too subjective. And, as Southern's story reminds us, there are undeniable risks in proposing imaginative explanations.

But Southern's example also teaches us something about the nature of history itself. As most readers will recognize after their first day of research, history does not present itself in readymade packages. There are always gaps, unexplained events, missing pieces of information. All authentic history writing, therefore, requires imaginative efforts to fill in the blank spaces where the evidence is mute or opaque. Part of being a historian is to take educated guesses, based on as much data as can be assembled, but venturing beyond it to explain. This venturing is where history writing becomes more than Sergeant Joe Friday's "just the facts ma'am" approach to crime solving. The humanness of the enterprise becomes apparent when we recognize that inevitably certain facts will seem more important than others because they connect to dominant interests of an individual historian. One or two dynamics will "naturally" seem more satisfying explanations than others because they mesh well with an author's worldview or previous experience.

Far from leaving us paralyzed by discovery of history's personal side, Southern's self-revelation demonstrates that history writing also includes an artistic dimension. Where the historian's imagination has not found some ordering insight, some focal point around which an entire account can be built, some sharp and vivid insight, then something other than history will result.

Does this mean that history writing is merely personal whim cut loose from all constraints? Hardly. Southern's third clue ("it worked") provides the key check on imagination run wild. Any explanation must be tested at the bar of known facts. While historians must move beyond data with their imaginations, they must also move back to their sources to see how well their theories work. If these sources contradict a given theory, then that theory must be revised. If an explanation leaves major elements of a plot out of the final story, then a historian will want to think twice before settling for it.

Distance

If imagination is an essential dimension of history writing, it is not the only one. Another is distance. By the time a historian has ransacked the archives, interviewed key people, identified intersecting plot lines, accounted for important contextual features, and determined the genius of a particular church or synagogue, congregational reality may be overwhelming. There is need, both in early stages of work and at the time when the written account is prepared, to step back and look for a bigger picture than can be seen from the midst of the notecards and transcripts.

Here the experience of a noted world historian can help. William H. McNeill relates a discovery made not in the library but on an afternoon walk. On a fourth of July during his graduate student days McNeill had climbed to Morningside Heights in New York City. He paused to watch the streams of traffic on the Henry Hudson Parkway below. Suddenly, it hit him: "to my amazement I observed that the stop-and-go traffic on the

Parkway constituted a longitudinal wave, with nodes and anti-nodes spaced at regular intervals, moving along the Parkway at a pace considerably faster than any single vehicle could make its way along the crowded roadway."

Lest McNeill's experience be dismissed as an afternoon's digression into gridlock studies on the part of an otherwise very serious historian, it is important to note that his version of world history is noted for its hypothesis of cultural or civilizational waves that have ebbed and flowed across the centuries. Thus his noting of a pattern on the parkway was quite in character. For him, wave-like patterns are sharp and vivid; they organize countless particular phenomena into larger processes.

Reflecting upon this discovery, McNeill expressed doubt that any of the drivers on the parkway had even the dimmest awareness that they were part of anything larger than their individual automobiles. Only the person who climbed to the proper distance — the observer from Morningside Heights — could discern the order in the chaos of modern commuting. It is imperative, McNeill suggests, that historians put themselves in positions where they can identify the processes and patterns of change which shape human existence. The primary contribution they make to their fellow human travellers is that periodically they step out of the flow of everyday life and attempt to discern what is really going on.

For congregational historians this means that part of the job is to step away from the archives and the thick reality of everyday parish life. Both in early research stages and at the time of preparing a final narrative it is necessary for a historian to put some distance between himself and his material. By stepping back to look for big pictures and large patterns, the historian does what no one else in the congregation has reason to do. Connections between seemingly unrelated events, recurring patterns, and major changes become visible when the congregation is viewed from a different, less immediate, perspective.

Audience

It seems self-evident, but it is important to remember that good authors know their audiences, and good books usually address distinct groups of people. Yet many projects stumble precisely at this self-evident point. Hours of research, piles of notecards, careful organization of material, and even creative leaps of imagination can be wasted if an author fails to write for someone in particular — not everyone in general.

For congregational historians the answer to the audience question will most often be Faith Lutheran Church, St. Vladimir's Parish, or whatever congregation has been the particular focus of study. While a few congregations may be written about because of community, denominational, or national interest, most will be studied for the sake of a synagogue or parish's own self-understanding. So the audience seems clear enough. And certainly there is plenty to do just to meet the needs of this primary audience.

To provide a sense of the past to people caught up in all the concerns of the present moment is a significant achievement. So is helping a collection of individuals who may have little or no sense of a common story to see their shared participation in a larger plot. Providing people with a picture of who they are, where they come from, what their successes and failures have been, can be a major contribution to a congregation that is unsure of itself. By taking these members on a metaphorical stroll along Morningside Heights the historian may help them see pattern and meaning where before they saw little connection between their lives and that of their congregation.

But pause for a moment and consider the consequences of writing exclusively for the current generation of church members. Will such a history be of any use to people in succeeding generations? Or is it likely to be referred to only by those people who can find their names on its pages? By catering to the interests of the current membership a history can quickly make itself obsolete, a poor return on a sizeable investment of time and energy. Perhaps one or two members of an envisioned audience should come from the grandchildren of the next generation!

One of the reasons for identifying plot lines that reach beyond a particular congregation is the recognition that congregational stories are usually much larger than most members realize. In a similar sense, attention to social context implies that congregations do not exist in airtight chambers designed to resist all contamination from their surrounding environments. On the contrary, they have an amazing number of relational links to the larger world, and many of those links can suggest additional audience members. For example, what about members of the local historical society? Or people interested in local forms of politics, ecumenism, or ethnicity? What could denominational historians or students of American religion learn from this congregation's history?

Answers to the audience question will depend upon local circumstances, congregational resources, and the ability of the individual author. But it is important to define the project's audience and then to convene the group as the writing proceeds. This can be done in one of two ways. A small editorial committee can be created to read early drafts and comment on what has been written. Such a device can be the source of many useful questions and suggestions. Or if it is not possible actually to assemble people, create a fictional committee and imagine its members — be specific about who they are! — reading over your shoulder as you reread your first and second drafts.

A word about publishing is in order here. To get all the way to the point of completing a final draft and then to fail to get it into print is an experience no author wants. Thus it is important to make publishing plans early and to tailor the final product to the agreed-upon specifications. In some cases congregations will decide to fund the printing costs out of their own resources and hire a printer for the project. In other cases a historian may be on his or her own. But in this age of computerized desktop publishing, it may turn out that publishing the history can be done with less difficulty than anyone imagined. Since such a large portion of our population is involved in knowledge dissemination it may be that the resources for publishing and editing are as close as the congregational directory. Other good leads include local printers, denominational printing houses, and local history associations.

Genre

The most important consideration in crafting the finished product is also the most difficult. In addition to historical imagination, proper distance, and a lively conversation with the intended audience, each writer needs to have a very clear idea about the nature of the product being crafted. Here an American church historian provides some essential advice.

In a speech to people interested in various aspects of congregational history, the late Ernest R. Sandeen divided the amalgam of products often loosely labeled "parish history" into five categories. Consideration of them can help clarify questions about the genre, or type of literary product that should emerge from the kind of inquiry we have been considering.

Sandeen labels his first category "the empty set" because the books that fit within it masquerade for history, telling stories of perfect churches and synagogues. In earlier times people wrote hagiographies, or quite stylized biographies of their saints. These embellished tales would sacrifice accuracy and completeness for the aura of perfection. Unfortunately, all too many local church histories mimic this "nothing bad ever happened here" fantasy. Their authors' desires to make no enemies result in stories that are more fiction than truth. Difficult moments in a congregation's experience — those occasions that test mettle and reveal character — are glossed over or ignored. For Sandeen such writing simply does not qualify as history.

Quite similar to the empty set is Sandeen's second type, the "devotional" book. Here the result is more of an extended prayer or meditation upon what God is doing in a particular congregation. Such reflections are an appropriate part of congregational life and Sandeen is not opposing them. However, he resists confusing sermonic exhortations or mission tracts with the category of history. History focuses on human subjects and purposes. There should be room in congregational histories — ample room — for the beliefs that various members hold about God and divine purpose. In fact, if these beliefs have not been considered at every phase of the project the distinctiveness of the congregation will most likely be missing from the final product. But history does not presume to speak from the divine point of view. So primary attention is given to the humans who do the believing and acting which creates, sustains, and, occasionally, destroys congregations.

Third is the "congregational yearbook" variety. These often come into being at significant anniversaries in a congregation's life. Such books are loaded with lists — of clergy, teachers, ushers, choir members, women's society members, and so on. While these collections can be very useful to the congregational historian, they are not to be confused with what Sandeen calls "genuine parish history." Lists and organizational calendars are only raw materials; they do not interpret, organize, and account for change in a congregation's life.

Ten years' worth of yearbooks yields a "chronicle," Sandeen's fourth category. Such super-lists can be extremely useful for producing congregational histories. They can include a rich assortment of pictures, sermons, membership data, portraits of old-time members and clergy. Frequently they provide hints of the "feeling tone" of a congregation at various points in its life. But they fall short. Yet, Sandeen mourns, the chronicle "is the most common form in which parish histories are written."

By now it should be clear that for Sandeen (and for me) these first four categories are pseudohistories, pretenders that fall short of category five, "genuine parish history." To merit inclusion in this category a book must be a piece of authentic historical scholarship. For Sandeen that means congregational history will tell readers more than who followed whom as pastor or synagogue president. He invites congregational historians to "express something about the real meaning of life." Their task is to take the experience of change seriously, to account for it, to press for its signficance. He warns against turning congregational history into congregational deception. Rather, the challenge is "to think seriously about what it means to live in community" in our modern context on the one hand and to help a particular congregation to "decide what it is that set you apart as a community" on the other.

Purpose

The goal of this book has been to provide a number of routes toward Sandeen's fifth category. One strategy toward reaching that goal was the introduction of different parish realities into the reader's consciousness. By describing a black Pentecostal church, a mainline suburban congregation, an inner-city Catholic parish, a rural Protestant church, a New England synagogue, and a number of other congregations, I hoped to raise questions for each reader about the distinctiveness of the particular congregation chosen for study. But I also sought to provide a number of angles of vision on any congregation through the different thematic thrusts of the various chapters.

By entering a congregation's life as a participant observer and searching for its distinctive genius, by taking seriously the ways in which a congregation is shaped by and shapes its context, by discerning a congregation's plot line, its character, worldview and ethos, a historian is doing much more than making lists. Instead, by artfully telling a story that takes change seriously, that sensitively relates major and minor characters, that looks for dramatic interruptions and subtle, almost invisible transitions, the historian is redirecting attention to a reality that has almost slipped from view in late twentieth-century America — the local place of worship. While they exist everywhere, they seem to be almost invisible, waiting for someone to take them seriously enough to demand our taking a fresh and serious look.

For Further Reading

R. W. Southern, "The Historical Experience," *Times Literary Supplement* (June 24, 1977), pp. 771-4.

William H. McNeill, *Mythistory and Other Essays* (Chicago: The University of Chicago Press, 1986). His experience on Morningside Heights is referred to on pp. 85-6.

Ernest R. Sandeen, "Congregational Histories as History," *The Church and History: A Guide for Archivists and Historians*, edited by Glenn W. Offerman (St. Paul, MN: Concordia College, 1981), pp. 2-13.

·8·

Reaching Beyond Nearby History

WHY TELL THE STORY OF A CONGREGATION? PEOPLE venture into writing the history of a place of worship for a variety of reasons. For some, a congregation is a cherished home world, a place rich in memories, a people full of traditions and meaningful associations. They can remember baptisms celebrated, marriages consecrated, funerals conducted, care received in front of this altar, at that font, or from one special individual. Generations of family history may be deeply inter-woven with the congregation's story; occasionally the monument in the congregation's cemetery or the plaque under a stained glass window may remind us of such deep associations. Often people gravitate toward one special pew which their family filled, at times fully and later, only partially. The wizened, white-haired widow who sits by herself in the sanctuary may have brought with her into that once full but now empty pew a host of people, now present only in her memory.

For others, a congregation may be a relatively new place, turned to after a move into town or a crisis in family or professional life. A pastor, priest, or rabbi may have been a pivotal figure at the time, a guide through turmoil and a door opener into a new community. At times of retirement of such pivotal people, or on anniversary occasions in a congregation's life, people sense that there is need to tell their story. Admiration, affection, and gratitude for special individuals often serve as initial motivators for people who become interested in congregational history.

But there are other reasons for telling a congregation's story, besides the obvious and important ones of personal association and loyalty. Some become interested in a congregation's history because of a longstanding curiosity or because they sense a formidable challenge which will provide both a sense of accomplishment and new perspective on themselves. In their willingness to take on the unknown, they resemble George Mallory, the English mountaineer, who when asked why he decided to become the first to attempt to scale Mt. Everest in 1921, snapped "Because it is there." Three years later, Mallory and a partner died on the Northeast Ridge of Everest without ever having reached the summit — a fate which may seem all too likely when one is staring at an unexplored mountain of congregational records in a cold church basement! Nonetheless, Mallory's terse explanation of his motives calls attention to the fact that there are some things that capture the imagination of individuals, that seem worth doing because of their own intrinsic worth. For Mallory it was a mountain that presented a challenge; for someone else it may be a cathedral, a temple, or a congregation.

Mallory's example also helps demonstrate that congregational history is not the private property of congregational members. Mallory, an Englishman, became interested in doing something that the native Sherpas who lived in the Himalayas did not feel was all that important. People interested in neighborhood or urban history, people who want to follow the development of various social movements such as temperance, feminism, integration, fundamentalism, or progressivism, or those seeking to understand the experience of a distinct ethnic group in America, may also find that in order to pursue their interests they may have to follow their questions into individual congregations.

Boston's Freedom Trail reminds all Americans who walk it that the revolutionary impulse which shaped our nation was often first expressed within church buildings, like Old North Church. The humble crypt of patriots John and Abigail Adams in the basement of First Unitarian Church in neighboring Quincy recalls that even the most dramatic and nonreligious actions in our nation's history frequently had congregational dimensions. That the Adams family chose to place the remains of their presidential forebearers in the basement of the church building in which they had worshipped is an indication that the Adams at least saw a connection.

People interested in secular institutions may often be surprised to find connections to congregations. The University of Chicago hardly seems to be an obvious example of an institution with congregational linkages. Notwithstanding its distinguished divinity school, the university has a secular image and most of its faculty and students would find the subject of its relationship to congregations to be at best a quaint subject. Yet its origins can be traced to several Baptist congregations in Chicago, most especially to Morgan Park Baptist Church, where the university's first president, William Rainey Harper, and several other key shapers worshipped and planned. But other major institutions like hospitals, benevolent agencies, and social organizations often have, or had, unrecognized congregational dimensions as well.

These primary reasons for writing congregational history are probably the ones that motivate most readers of this book. On the pages that follow, however, I would like to suggest seven additional incentives that demonstrate that congregational history involves larger, more universal issues than those normally associated with one congregation's limited horizon.

The Larger Values of Congregational History

1. Congregational behavior is one of the oldest and most enduring forms of human activity. Max Weber, the great German sociologist who first named and described the "Protestant Ethic," was also an observer of modern congregations. In fact, he concluded that the Puritans, Pietists, and other religious groups which inhabited the cities of Europe during the post-Reformation period, had developed a new congregational style which reflected the needs of an emerging "middle class." The people who assembled in these new religious institutions reflected a "tendency toward affiliation with an ethical, rational, congregational religion . . . more apt to be found the closer one gets to those classes which have been the carriers of modern rational productive economic activity." For Weber then, congregations, especially the Protestant versions which emerged as voluntary communities distinct from state-sponsored churches, were something new.

Weber's assertion of the novelty of the modern congregational form, however, cannot be allowed to conceal an equally important fact. While the form may be relatively new, the congregational phenomenon is ancient. Archaeologists' shovels keep turning up traces of earlier instances of religious gathering. The great historian of religion, the late Mircea Eliade, began his magisterial summation of the development of religious ideas across the cultures and centuries of the world with a consideration of some of that archaeological data — burial remains from the Paleanthropian age (400,000–300,000 B.C.E.). Although these fragmentary traces do not permit a reconstruction of the beliefs which have long since vanished from human memory, evidence of the careful arrangement of human bones provides the earliest sign of human gathering for the religious purposes of responding to death and interpreting its meaning. The cave art at Lascaux, France (15,000–13,000 B.C.E.), the skulls found beneath the floors of houses in ancient Jericho (ca. 6770 B.C.E.) and the great megaliths of Stonehenge (4000–1900 B.C.E.) silently bear witness to the varieties of ways and places employed by prehistoric peoples when they gathered for religious reasons.

The tension created by placing descriptions of "new" and "ancient" congregational behavior next to each other is a useful one. On the one hand, most congregational historians will be dealing with material from modern congregational life, the kind that Weber identified. But on the other hand, every explorer of congregational history ventures into a realm of human behavior which seems to be almost as old as the human species. The life of people in the places of worship of our time thus provides opportunity for learning about recent developments in one of the oldest human endeavors. And we need to be careful not to repeat the mistakes of the past. As self-evident as much of the congregational behavior of our day may seem to us, unless it is described and interpreted by current observers, much of it will be lost forever.

2. Congregations serve as windows into zones of modern life which are otherwise remote and inaccessible. There are many reasons for opening these congregational windows. For most of this century scholars have recognized that official documents, the reflections of elites, and the artifacts which come to be valued as "high culture" are, by themselves, insufficient to provide adequate understanding of human history. Whole realms of life are left out of view when only great men and women and their creations are considered.

The modern social sciences — sociology, anthropology, psychology, economics — have emerged to call attention to important dimensions of human experience which previously went unnoticed. Clearly, the variety of academic disciplines which crowd the college and university curricula of our land serve to redirect our age's attention beyond official positions, the pronouncements of recognized spokespersons, or any solitary individual's preferred "short list" of interesting subjects.

Oddly enough, few people seem to have noticed how strategically located congregations are to provide access to these more illusive but increasingly important dimensions of life. Congregations are places where people bring together their most cherished aspirations and their everyday existence. Within their walls fundamental beliefs about God and the world intermingle with ethnic holiday traditions and images of the American way of life. Although they are often assumed to be islands of dreary conformity and blandness, America's congregations are in fact busy intersections for many of the main pathways of the nation's life. Denominational labels notwithstanding, congregations teem with the reality of modern pluralism, as innumerable traditions, ways of life, beliefs and values are brought together by members who come from varying ethnic, social, educational, economic and religious backgrounds.

It is in congregations that many people discuss pressing concerns such as the education of their children, the needs of the homeless, questions about serious ethical issues like the legality of abortion or the morality of withholding food and water from terminally ill parents. In private conversations and in public forums congregation members express and form opinions on national policy vis-a-vis an oppressive Third World regime or the menace of the nuclear buildup.

Often these members participate in a great but unnoticed conflict of interpretations. For example, one may eavesdrop on a congregational meeting where concern about adolescent drug use is expressed by Bible-quoting, cigarette-smoking parents. They want their church to compete with the youth culture that lures their children through the media, the advertisers, and the rock musicians of the moment. The astute observer will find rich contradictions in well-intentioned and often quite religiously based protests against adolescent conformism by parents who happen to have little animals embroidered on their sweaters or designer labels on their jeans.

Few other institutions in our land can rival congregations in their role as repositories for a seemingly endless variety of official and operative beliefs, formal and informal behaviors. Where else do people so clearly express the collective representations of reality they share, the memories, hopes, fears, anxieties, and crises that shape who they are? It is in these institutions that one can find first signs of great sea changes in attitudes and perceptions about so many aspects of life. Early expressions of new beliefs and desires regularly collide with strong reactions, fears, and countermovements. For example, women have both experimented with new roles and found doors closed to them in congregations. In congregational gossip or in the private conversation between anguished individuals and their clergy, questions about changing sexual mores have often surfaced long before becoming visible in other places in the culture.

In short, places of worship provide astute inquirers with thick slices of life — excellent observation platforms from which to watch how individuals, their beliefs and practices, their neighborhoods and communities change. Even the most colorless data in a congregation's past can contain a rich story. For example, behind the dry figures of a church budget are congregational decisions which often reflect the economic assumptions of American capitalism as much as they do the economics of Jesus or those of post-Exilic Judaism. While it is easy to claim too much for the study of congregations, it is also hard to imagine any institution which offers more of American life to the observer who knows what to look for.

3. We have attempted to understand religion in America without paying attention to one of its most fundamental institutions. The study of religion in America is a large industry. There are 201 seminaries which belong to the Association of Theological Schools in the United States and Canada, each boasting a faculty of experts on the many subjects considered essential for preparing future clergy. In addition there are more than 900 departments of religious studies in the various universities and colleges throughout the land. Each of those departments, in turn, has its own set of experts, many of whom are devoted to types of religious inquiry that seminaries overlook or consider luxuries. Yet with all of these institutions and experts devoted to the study of religion in all of its dimensions, it is amazing how unstudied congregations have been.

The scholarly imperatives of distinct academic disciplines provide partial explanation for the lack of attention to individual congregations. Biblical scholars have sacred texts to master; church historians focus upon denominations and official church documents; ethicists isolate individual or social problems for analysis; and practical theologians concentrate on the various professional skills needed by clergy. Religious studies experts venture into exotic religions, or probe classic religious texts and figures with their students. The reigning questions of their various specialties impel few toward congregations, and no clamor is heard for books which probe actual congregational life. The literature which has emerged offered, for the most part, recipes for reshaping congregations rather than studies of them.

In addition, the rapid proliferation of new social, intellectual, political and international problems in the past century has also helped deflect attention from congregations. In the face of shattering modern experiences like the Holocaust or Hiroshima, in the midst of first encounters with new social realities like those met in the turbulent 1960s, in the presence of great intellectual challenges presented by epoch shapers such as Darwin, Freud, Einstein and Marx, congregations seemed to merit little space on the crowded agenda of scholars of religion.

Occasionally a few scholars have turned their attention to congregations, but their efforts have largely been exceptional and episodic. H. Paul Douglass and Edmund deS. Brunner, for example, gave congregations a prominent place on the research agenda of their Institute of Social and Religious Research during its thirteen-year career. But after the Institute closed its doors in 1934, little sustained inquiry into congregations occurred. Not until the mid 1970s did serious momentum develop in a new field of research which came to be called "congregational studies."

For the most part, the only people — aside from the exceptions just alluded to — willing to study the congregations of the land were members who lived in them and who wanted to preserve their heritage. While professional scholars looked elsewhere, numerous armchair historians and devoted members attempted to preserve their heritages. Most of their efforts resulted in anniversary volumes, scrapbooks, chronicles, and archives which went virtually unnoticed by the scholars, and, all too often, by denominational and congregational leaders as well. Exceptions to this pattern of ignorance about congregational life were the efforts by some enlightened denominational archivists to assemble collections of congregational materials and to assist congregations in building their own archives. But, outside of the handful of scholars who studied a few congregations for specific research projects, the denominational archivists and the local historians who wrote about their congregations because they were there and important to them, congregations remained the great unnoticed resource for students of religion.

4. There has been a bias against congregations in American life which

has kept people from taking them seriously. Douglass and Brunner, the two scholars who led the most significant effort to study North American congregations in the early part of the century, were also among the first to identify the bias against them. In 1935, they published *The Protestant Church as a Social Institution* which reported on what they believed to be "the largest body of objective research of its kind." In addition to presenting an enormous amount of data about Protestant congregations, they called attention to "a considerable body of Protestant opinion which has reached a highly unfavorable estimate of the religious values of the present church." There was a pervasive "burnt-finger attitude" on the part of many who tried to reform these institutions and a tendency to make them the collective "Protestant whipping boy" responsible for all the woes which affected religious groups during the Great Depression. Actually, before the twentieth century had begun leaders of the Social Gospel movement had criticized congregations for failing to meet the challenges of modern urban America. What Douglass and Brunner had done was to name an attitude which pre-existed their studies and characterized much subsequent thinking about congregations.

The pervasiveness of the burnt-finger attitude became apparent in numerous attempts by religious leaders and reformers to build alternatives to congregations during the middle years of this century. The Harlem Parish Project, the Detroit Industrial Ministry, the Schaumburg Village Apartment House Ministry and the experimental coffee house and retreat ministry of the Church of the Savior in Washington, D.C., were just a few examples of what Sydney Ahlstrom termed a "tidal wave of questioning of all the traditional structures of Christendom, above all, of the so-called parish church."

The chorus of critics who assailed the "whipping boy" included some of America's leading scholars of religion. Peter Berger, for example, argued in his *Noise of the Solemn Assemblies* that congregations helped keep religion irrelevant to the dominant issues and powers of the age. They created background noise which served to distract people from what really mattered. Another critic, Gibson Winter, indicated his disapproval of the preoccupations of modern congregations in his *The Suburban Captivity of the Churches*.

No wonder congregations received little attention! A prevailing mindset about congregations assumed they were irrelevant, relics of a past age, a source of religion's trouble in modern times. It seemed all too obvious that very little of interest or use could be found in them. And one does not have to look very far to find signs of that mindset today.

5. Even though their irrelevance has been assumed, congregations have in fact held a strategic location at the boundary of the public and private spheres of modern life. One of the leading assumptions of the modern era has been that life *is* divided into public and private realms. That assumption was codified in the First Amendment to the U.S. Constitution which decreed that "Congress shall make no law respecting an establishment of religion, or prohibiting the free exercise thereof." From the time of Enlightenment figures like Thomas Jefferson and James Madison onward, the United States has adopted a style which recognizes a line of separation between the public realm of government and law and the private world of home and opinion. In order to create a nation which could accommodate people from many faiths, the founders relegated religion to the private sphere, the zone of opinion. While religious leaders were allowed to play public roles, and while religion frequently impelled people into the public sphere for the purpose of furthering cherished causes like abolition, temperance, or public health, there was no designated place for religion to assume in the nation's public discourse.

But it has become clear that congregations have not been merely private institutions in the same sense that someone's home might be. While denominational beliefs often provided a sacred canopy under which many people might gather, it was obvious that people brought a variety of opinions with them into their congregations. The countless conflicts recorded in congregational minutes can be seen as indicators of the fact that from the very beginning these institutions shared in the larger public problems which had concerned the founders. Congregations became places where people struggled to find points of agreement between differing opinions just as legislatures and public meetings did.

What's more, they became, as James Luther Adams has noted, important places where people learned the "voluntary principle" which is close to the heart of the American style. In congregations people learned to listen to appeals, to think for themselves, to form groups which could deal with specific programs. In that sense, they often served and continue to serve as nurseries which form people for public life, providing first exposures to the problems and patterns of behavior that characterize public life.

In addition to providing experiences that help equip people for participation in the public sphere, congregations serve as strategic mediators between the two zones of life. In a somewhat more affirming assessment than the one referred to earlier, Peter Berger joined Richard John Neuhaus in pointing out that congregations are "mediating structures" which connect to both public and private spheres. Although they are not the only such institutions, congregations are places where people express private beliefs and opinions in a context with a public dimension. Congregations are way stations on the road between private worlds and the larger public arena. In them people learn how to relate deeply held religious beliefs to questions that have a public character. They are places for forming, testing, and revising opinions. They are also places for launching public movements and challenging complacent private worlds with new questions and concerns.

Only a handful of people have paid attention to this distinctive public–private character of the congregation. Part of the silence about this aspect of congregational life is due to several of the factors previously mentioned, like the bias against congregations and the lack of critical thinking about them. But another reason has to do with the modern attempt to separate private and public worlds. There is constant pressure on both sides of the divide to spill over. Issues of public life touch upon deep private beliefs. And people with deeply held religious perspectives constantly seek to make a difference in life outside the private sphere. Because no one can be exactly certain just where the line between public and private actually exists, there has been a tendency to assume that congregations are always on the private side. Yet a careful reading of our nation's history indicates that again and again congregations served as places of connection between the two. To fully understand our nation's public struggle over temperance or civil rights, for example, one needs to know something about the congregations which shaped leaders like Frances Willard or Martin Luther King, Jr., and their followers.

6. Developments within the field of history make congregations natural places to turn for new knowledge about modern Americans. In 1931, Carl Becker, a distinguished historian at Cornell University, used his presidential address to the American Historical Association to

identify similarities between professional historians and everybody else who migrated through the modern world. So pervasive had modern pragmatic historical ways of thinking become that Becker titled his essay "Everyman his own historian."

In order to negotiate successfully the many turns of twentieth-century life, Becker claimed that people employed the historian's techniques of "recalling things said and done," searching for previously unknown facts, and critically comparing various accounts of situations to sift error from truth. Those operations, he claimed, were as necessary for paying the coal bill as for tracing the origins of the Declaration of Independence. Simply put, no matter where a person might turn, evidence of a much older and a much more related world awaited both the professional scholar and the sensitive observer. Fossils and tarpits, archaeological excavations and newly discovered manuscripts regularly pushed back estimates of the age of the world or the origins of the human species. Further, the modern university with all of its departments of study revealed an interdependent and more complex world than the one imagined by the majority of humans before the advent of the Darwinian, Einsteinian, and Marxian revolutions. Conventional cause-and-effect explanations which had worked for centuries rapidly became obsolete in an era of complexity and layers of meaning.

Each person needed to become aware of the climate of opinion which shaped how people in a given culture, period, or social setting perceived, believed, and acted. In order to help people find their way in this new history-laden environment, Becker's aphorism pointed to the need for each person, not merely the professional inhabitants of seminars and library carrels, to become a historian, an individual aware of his or her situation in a complex web of events, ideas, circumstances, and shaping factors. In other words, to live in an age dominated by historical realities and historical ways of thinking, people needed to master history, to put its methods and perspectives to work for themselves.

Becker's advice is still timely. Now more than a half century after his important essay, one has only to scan the offerings of the nation's public television stations (and to a lesser extent the network offerings of the commercial broadcasters) to see how much interest there is in earlier chapters of human history and even the most remote cultures and peoples. The explosion of historical knowledge in the last century has made available ranges of human experience which few could have imagined even in Becker's day. New areas of inquiry like the experience of women, the family, and ethnic groups have found room on the history shelves along with other more "popular" topics like sports, forms of entertainment, and media.

No longer can history be written only about the once conventional topics of wars, presidents, inventions, and discoveries. And there is little sign of a let-up in the historical imperative to know more about all areas of human life. Within the realm of scholarly or academic history writing, the phrase "social history" has become the shorthand expression to describe this shift in the subject matter and method of history. In essence the direction of history writing has reversed. What was once primarily a "trickle down" discipline which focused on the exceptional individual, event, or idea and the way in which he, she, or it made a difference in subsequent history, has become a "bubble up" pursuit, which seeks to mine everyday life, common people, and routine events for the contextual structures and factors which can help account for something as complex as the emergence of the sixteenth-century Reformation or the success of the American Revolution.

One example of this shift in historical thinking is the emergence of interest in what David E. Kyvig and Myron A. Marty have named *nearby history*. For Kyvig and Marty *nearby history* includes "the entire range of possibilities in a person's immediate environment." They want to exploit the new capabilities present in "computers and quantitative techniques to identify economic, social, political, and growth patterns of families and communities, thus developing a much fuller and more accurate picture of American society from the bottom up." In their estimation nearby history is "public" history, a type of inquiry and writing which helps people better understand, explain, and interpret the close-at-hand primary worlds where they spend most of their time.

This type of history is becoming increasingly attractive to professional scholars, but the range of possible subjects is too great for them to cover. The "emerging field" of nearby history, which includes congregational history, requires a growing cohort of inquirers who can work with what is immediately at hand.

These developments in "secular" history have their parrallels in the field of American religious history. In *A Nation of Behavers*, Martin E. Marty described four approaches or "maps" which have been used by historians who have sought to master the American religious landscape.

The first map, most in vogue during the colonial era of North America, located American religion on the basis of theology and geography. Seventeenth-century New England, for example, was seen as a place where Puritans of various stripes contended over preferred interpretations of covenant theology. Quakers, continental pietists, and others who sought space to erect their own religious and ethnic communities divided the middle colonies among themselves.

As the colonies came together to form a new nation, and as established churches like the Anglicans of Virginia yielded their privileged status a new denominational approach to history writing emerged. During the era of nation building, histories of expanding, competing, cooperating, and pioneering groups of Presbyterians, Lutherans, Episcopalians, and Methodists began to appear.

This denominational approach to thinking about and reporting religious history dominated the discipline of "church history" until the United States replaced its small-town visage with a new urban face — the face of pluralism, industrialization, new wealth, and new social problems — in the late nineteenth century. Then what Marty described as the third map became necessary. In the new circumstances of the twentieth century, scholars like Will Herberg began to track cleavages and commonalties within and across the denominations. Political issues like temperance, slavery, women's rights, labor legislation, and social welfare quickly blurred the neat lines of denominational America. Historians began to follow reform movements, or major social problems in and out of various religious groups. Social scientists began to find evidence of religious pluralism not only between denominations but within them.

No longer could all the members of one Presbyterian denomination be assumed to think the same way about creedal statements or social issues. Visible differences of belief about major doctrinal affirmations such as the creation of the world, the nature and character of the Scriptures, life after death, or the possibility of salvation outside of a particular religious community revealed the limitations of the denominational map. So did social issues like integration, shifting sexual mores, or controversial foreign-policy decisions like those which surrounded United States' involvement in the Vietnam War.

Marty's fourth map is an "emerging paradigm" which is also a "species of social history." If the first three types of maps concentrated on religious ideas, religious institutions, and religious politics, respectively, this map seeks to track religious social behavior. In his own attempt to redraw the American religious map, Marty found that locating people in one or more of six religious-behavioral zones discussed in chapter 6 (Mainline, Evangelical/Fundamentalist, Pentecostal–Charismatic, New, Ethnic, and Civil) often was more useful than a denominational tag, or the liberal/conservative label.

If both secular and religious history are turning toward what has been called "people's history," if the daily practices and beliefs of ordinary people are becoming more necessary for understanding the sources, direction, and fabric of modern life, if more and more people want and need to know more about their nearby past, then the congregations of the land seem obvious places to turn. Another of America's leading historians, Oscar Handlin sensed this need when he wrote a foreword to the history of Temple Israel mentioned in chapter 6. "American religious institutions have not in the past received the serious study they deserve," he wrote. But lest he sound like a champion of the denominational approach described by Marty he quickly went on. "There are books enough that deal with the careers of the leaders, and there are numerous accounts of theology. But there has been little effort to probe the nature of the social forms that give meaning and order to the faith of the mass of people."

Handlin deplored the self-congratulatory commemorative volumes which often pass as congregational history. He called for serious efforts at "self-comprehension" by people in the congregations of the land. Recognizing that the diversity of American religious life made reliance upon experts an unrealistic solution, Handlin dared to hope that "communicants themselves (would) acquire the capacity to write about themselves with candor and detachment." Now, more than thirty years after Handlin identified the need for congregational historians, his diagnosis remains sound. Only if people within congregations gain this ability to understand themselves will the rest of our society begin to grasp the signficiance of the past that these institutions and their members possess.

7. Congregational history can help congregations find their identities in a pluralistic and rapidly changing context. Not everyone who becomes interested in this variety of *nearby history* will be concerned with how the study of a congregation's past can contribute to that institution's ongoing life. Some, for instance, may probe a congregation in

order to understand why this building stands on this corner, or how that group of people helped shape a given social movement. But many, indeed most, of those who conduct such an inquiry will be concerned about the future of the congregations they examine and describe. Often they will be writing at moments of transition in congregational life: at the end of an important pastorate, at the beginning of a second century, at a time when a generation of members begins to disappear in the face of social change or the steady progression of years.

This concern about the future can lead to hesitancy about disclosing skeletons found in the archives and blemishes uncovered beneath the congregation's smooth surface. Sometimes a close friend or a favored organization will be found to have another side or a different face than the one most people saw. Should a historian "go public" about such things, or is it better to bury damning evidence in a file folder at the back of a drawer? The answer depends upon the purpose the historian brings to the material. If the purpose is to flaunt any example of hypocrisy in a group's life, then it is safe to assume that every piece of unflattering material will find its way into the final draft of the history. On the other hand, if back-slapping and creating a warm cocoon of good feeling are the goals, then it is likely that such moments will never be revisited.

A third, and more appropriate, purpose is to help a congregation discover a truer sense of its identity. The historian's task is not to invent a preferred identity for the congregation, nor to reinforce a partial one. Instead, the goal is to describe and reconstruct the full identity of a congregation, to show how it developed, changed, wavered, and reasserted itself through its years of life.

Why stress identity? Modern life poses the identity question in very powerful ways. Unlike medieval or ancient peoples, moderns have to labor at defining who they are. Psychoanalysts and sociologists have written an overwhelming number of books which examine the ways in which modernity continually forces people to grapple with the "Who am I?" question. The search for identity is a recurring theme in modern literature and art, and whole industries have arisen to provide materials and therapies for those who feel the pressure of the identity quest.

It is not too bold to suggest that institutions as well as individuals go through struggles to discern and clarify identity. One can read American religious history, for example, as an ongoing quest by each religious group that dwells in this promising land to maintain its identity in the face of all that threatens to overwhelm it. New ideas, new types of people, new ways of life, new social problems all converged upon those who tried the American experiment. As America's religious denominations formed, divided, regrouped, merged, and cooperated they were searching for their own identities in the midst of all their other concerns.

No less is true of congregations. In order to survive in America they were forced to co-exist with all the other varieties of religious experience and organization that make this land so colorful. With each new congregation member came new beliefs, new social worlds, new problems. Their leaders often brought new models of communal life and revised understandings of central teachings which jostled cherished ways. Long-time members followed modern migratory patterns of career paths, higher education, and suburbanization. The result has been the involvement of most congregations in an unending struggle to define themselves.

The congregational historian can make an important contribution to individuals and congregations searching for who they are. By probing the past and relating it to the present life of the congregation the historian can help people recover the traditions which shaped their forebearers. A longer memory can be provided, one which enables people to let go of the passing fads that parade as traditions but lack the depth to root people and connect them to durable systems of meaning. In addition, the congregational historian can help people identify the places where identities have broken down, where traditions have been lost, where dramatic or subtle changes have occurred in past times that have set the terms for how this generation perceives itself and its world. Perhaps by looking back at their histories, individuals and congregations can rediscover their moorings and be enabled to set off in directions which will give future historians of *places of worship* richer, fuller, and more complete stories to tell.

For Further Reading

Max Weber's *The Sociology of Religion*, is excerpted in Max Weber, *On Charisma and Institution Building: Selected Papers*, edited by S.N. Eisenstadt (Chicago: University of Chicago Press, 1968). His discussion of the new congregational form for modernity occurs at p. 292.

Mircea Eliade, *A History of Religious Ideas:. From the Stone Age to the Eleusinian Mysteries*, translated by Willard R. Trask, Vol. 1 (Chicago: University of Chicago Press, 1978), especially pp. 9, 15-19, 44, 118, 121-122.

H. Paul Douglass and Edmund deS. Brunner, *The Protestant Church as a Social Institution* (New York: Harper and Brothers, 1935). Note especially pp. v-vii, 3-30.

Sydney Ahlstrom's assessment of the modern parish is in *A Religious History of the American People*, Vol. 2 (Garden City, New York: Image Books, 1975), p. 604.

Peter L. Berger, *The Noise of the Solemn Assemblies* (Garden City, New York: Doubleday and Company, 1961).

Gibson Winter, *The Suburban Captivity of the Churches* (Garden City, New York: Doubleday and Company, 1961).

James Luther Adams, "The Voluntary Principle in the Forming of American Religion," *The Religion of the Republic*, edited by Elwyn A. Smith (Philadelphia: Fortress Press, 1971), pp. 217-246.

Peter L. Berger and Richard John Neuhaus, *To Empower People: The Role of Mediating Structures in Public Policy* (Washington, D.C.: American Enterprise Institute for Public Policy Research, 1977).

Carl A. Becker, *Everyman His Own Historian* (New York: F. S. Croft & Co., Inc, 1935), pp. 233-55.

David E. Kyvig and Myron A. Marty, *Nearby History: Exploring the Past Around You* (Nashville: The American Association for State and Local History), especially pp. 10-11.

Martin E. Marty, *A Nation of Behavers* (Chicago: The University of Chicago Press, 1976).

Oscar Handlin's remarks are in the foreword to Arthur Mann, editor, *Growth and Achievement: Temple Israel, 1854-1954* (Cambridge, Mass.: The Riverside Press, 1954), pp. vii-viii.

Appendix A
Bibliographic Starting Points

THE LITERATURE ON AMERICAN RELIGION IS IMMENSE, growing, and uneven. The listing of titles offered here does not pretend to do justice to this enormous field of study. Instead it seeks to offer places for historians to begin searches that can add significant dimensions to their projects. All scholars have preferred "canons" or lists of texts that they turn to for help. Thus many experts may suggest different titles than those listed here. And those suggestions should be followed! But these titles do provide starting points. Titles were selected in view of helpfulness as general introductions and overviews of important themes, movements, and denominations in American religion. Where possible, more recent titles have been chosen over more dated ones, while the texts mentioned in the preceding chapters are not repeated.

I.   GENERAL INTRODUCTIONS TO NORTH AMERICAN
      RELIGION AND BIBLIOGRAPHIC SOURCES:

UNITED STATES

Burr, Nelson R., ed. *Religion in American Life.* Goldentree Bibliographies in American History. New York: Appleton-Century-Crofts, 1971.

Gaustad, Edwin S. *Historical Atlas of Religion in America.* Rev. ed. New York: Harper and Row, 1976.

_____, ed. *A Documentary History of Religion in America.* 2 vols. Grand Rapids, Mich.: Eerdmans, 1982-83.

Handy, Robert T. *A History of the Churches in the United States and Canada.* Oxford: Clarendon Press, 1976.

Hudson, Winthrop S. *Religion in America.* 2nd ed. New York: Charles Scribner's Sons, 1972.

James, Gilbert and Wickens, Robert G., eds. *The Town and Country Church: A Topical Bibliography*. Wilmore, Ky.: Department of the Church in Society, Asbury Theological Seminary, 1968.

Lippy, Charles and Williams, Peter, eds. *Encyclopedia of American Religion*. 3 vols. Westport, Conn.: Greenwood Press, 1987

Noll, Mark A. and Hatch, Nathan O., eds. *Eerdman's Handbook to the History of Christianity in America*. Grand Rapids, Mich.: Eerdmans, 1983.

Piepkorn, Arthur Carl. *Profiles in Belief: The Religious Bodies of the United States and Canada*. New York: Harper and Row, 1977.

CANADA

Grant, John Webster, gen. ed. *A History of the Christian Church in Canada*. 3 vols. Toronto: Ryerson Press, 1966-72.

_____, ed. *The Churches and the Canadian Experience*. Toronto: Ryerson Press, 1963.

Handy, Robert T. *A History of the Churches in the United States and Canada*. Oxford: Clarendon Press, 1976.

Kilbourn, William; Forrest, A.C.; and Watson, Patrick. *Religion in Canada: The Spiritual Development of a Nation*. Toronto: McClelland & Stewart, 1968.

II.   SPECIFIC DENOMINATIONAL HISTORIES:

AFRICAN METHODIST EPISCOPAL

Richardson, Harry V. *Dark Salvation: The Story of Methodism as it Developed Among Blacks in America*. Garden City, N.Y.: Anchor Press, 1976.

AFRICAN METHODIST EPISCOPAL ZION

Walls, William J. *The African Methodist Episcopal Zion Church: Reality of the Black Church*. Charlotte, N.C.: AME Zion Publishers, 1974.

BAPTIST

Baker, Robert Andrew. *Relations Between Northern and Southern Baptists*. New York: Arno Press, 1948.

_____. *The Southern Baptist Convention and its*

People, 1607-1972. Nashville: Broadman Press, 1974.

Eighmy, John. *Churches in Cultural Captivity: a History of the Social Attitudes of Southern Baptists*. Rev. ed. Knoxville, Tenn.: University of Tennessee Press, 1978.

Encyclopedia of Southern Baptists. 5 vols. Nashville: Broadman Press, 1958.

Spain, Rufus. *At Ease in Zion: A Social History of Southern Baptists, 1865-1900*. Nashville: Vanderbilt University Press, 1967.

Starr, Edward C. *A Baptist Bibliography*. 25 vols. Rochester, N.Y.: American Baptist Historical Society, 1947-1976.

Torbet, Robert G. *A History of the Baptists*. 4th ed., rev. Valley Forge, Penn.: Judson Press, 1975.

Torbet, Robert G. and Hill, Samuel S., Jr. *Baptists: North and South*. Valley Forge, Penn.: Judson Press, 1964.

CHRISTIAN CHURCH (DISCIPLES OF CHRIST)

Beazely, George C., Jr., ed. *The Christian Church (Disciples of Christ): An Interpretive Examination in the Cultural Context*. St. Louis: Bethany Press, 1973.

Harrell, David E., Jr. *Quest for the Christian America: The Disciples of Christ and American Society to 1866*. Nashville, Tenn.: Disciples of Christ Historical Society, 1966.

_____. *The Social Sources of Division in the Disciples of Christ, 1865-1900*. Atlanta: Publishing Systems, 1973.

McAllister, Lester G. and Tucker, William E. *Journey in Faith*. St. Louis: Bethany Press, 1975.

CHRISTIAN SCIENCE

Braden, Charles S. *Christian Science Today: Power, Policy, Practice*. Dallas: Southern Methodist University Press, 1958.

Gottschalk, Stephen. *The Emergence of Christian Science in American Religious Life*. Berkeley, Cal.: University of California Press, 1973.

Peel, Robert. *Christian Science: Its Encounter with American Culture*. New York: Holt, 1958.

_____. *Mary Baker Eddy: The Years of Discovery, The Years of Trial, The Years of Authority*. 3 vols. New York: Holt, Rinehart & Winston, 1966-1977.

CHURCHES OF CHRIST
see also CHRISTIAN CHURCH
(DISCIPLES OF CHRIST)

West, Earl I. *The Search for the Ancient Order.* 2 vols. Indianapolis: Religious Book Service, 1950.

CHURCH OF GOD IN CHRIST

Cornelius, Lucille. *The Pioneer History of the Church of God in Christ.* Memphis, Tenn.: GOGIC Publishing House, 1975.

Please, Charles H. *Fifty Years of Achievement: Church of God in Christ.* Memphis, Tenn.: COGIC Publishing House, n.d.

CHURCH OF JESUS CHRIST OF THE
LATTER DAY SAINTS (THE MORMONS)
Including
REORGANIZED CHURCH OF JESUS CHRIST
OF THE LATTER DAY SAINTS

Allen, James B. and Leonard, Glen M. *The Story of the Latter Day Saints.* Salt Lake City: Deseret Book Co. in collaboration with the History Department of the Church of Jesus Christ of the Latter Day Saints, 1976.

Blair, Alma R. "Reorganized Church of Christ of Latter Day Saints: Moderate Mormonism." *The Restoration Movement: Essays in Mormon History.* McKiernan, F. Mark; Blair, Alma R.; and Edwards, Paul M.; eds. Lawrence, Kan: Coronado Press, 1973.

Hensen, Klaus J. *Mormonism and the American Experience.* Chicago: University of Chicago Press, 1981.

Shipps, Jan. *Mormonism: The Story of a New Religious Tradition.* Urbana, Ill.; University of Illinois Press, 1984.

CHURCH OF THE BRETHREN

Bittenger, Emmert F. *Heritage and Promise: Perspective on the Church of the Brethren,* Rev. ed. Elgin, Ill.: Brethren Press, 1983.

The Brethren Encyclopedia. 3 vols. Philadelphia: Brethren Encyclopedia, Inc., 1983-4.

Durnbaugh, Donald, ed. *Church of the Brethren: Yesterday and Today.* Elgin, Ill.: Brethren Press, 1986.

COLORED/CHRISTIAN METHODIST EPISCOPAL CHURCH

Lakey, Orthal H. *Rise of "Colored Methodism": a Study of the Background and the Beginnings of the Christian Methodist Episcopal Church.* Dallas: Crescendo Book Publications, 1972.

Phillips, Charles Henry. *History of the Colored Methodist Episcopal Church in America: Comprising its Organization, Subsequent Developments and Present Status.* 1898. Salem, N.H.: Ayer Co. Publishers, 1972.

CONGREGATIONALIST
see UNITED CHURCH OF CHRIST

EASTERN ORTHODOX/GREEK ORTHODOX

Bogolepov, Alexander A. *Toward an American Orthodox Church: The Establishment of an Autocephalous Orthodox Church.* New York: Morehouse-Barlow, 1963.

Calian, C. Samuel. *Icon and Pulpit: The Protestant-Orthodox Encounter.* Philadelphia: Westminster Press, 1968.

Constantelos, Demetrios, J. *Understanding the Greek Orthodox Church: Faith, History, and Practice.* New York: Seabury Press, 1982.

Ware, Timothy. *The Orthodox Church.* New York: Penguin Books, 1963.

EPISCOPAL

Albright, Raymond W. *History of the Protestant Episcopal Church.* New York: Macmillan, 1964.

Booty, John E. *The Church in History.* The Church's Teaching Series, vol. 3. New York: Seabury, 1973.

EVANGELICAL AND REFORM
see UNITED CHURCH OF CHRIST

ISLAM

The Encyclopedia of Islam. New edition. Leiden: E. J. Brill, 1979.

Essien-Udom, E. U. *Black Nationalism: A Search for an Identity in America.* Chicago: University of Chicago Press, 1962.

Lincoln, C. Eric. *The Black Muslims in America.* Rev. ed. Westport, Conn.: Greenwood Press, 1973.

Orfalea, Gregory. *Before the Flames: A Quest for the History of Arab Americans.* Austin, Tex.: University of Texas Press, 1988.

JEHOVAH'S WITNESSES

Sterling, Chandler W. *The Witnesses: One God, One Victory.* Chicago: Regency, 1975.

Stroup, Herbert Hewitt. *The Jehovah's Witnesses.* 1945. Reprint. New York: Russell and Russell, 1967.

Whalen, William. *Armageddon Around the Corner: A Report on the Jehovah's Witnesses.* New York: John Day Co., 1962.

JUDAISM

American Jewish Yearbook. Vols. 1-50. Philadelphia: The Jewish Publication Society of America, 1899/1900-. Vols. 51-88. New York: The American Jewish Committee, 1951-.

Blau, Joseph Leon. *Judaism in America: From Curiosity to Third Faith.* Chicago: University of Chicago Press, 1976.

Encyclopedia Judaica. 16 vols. Jerusalem: Keter Publishing House, Ltd., 1972.

Glazer, Nathan. *American Judaism.* 2nd ed. Chicago: University of Chicago Press, 1972.

Jick, Leon A. *The Americanization of the Synagogue, 1820-1870.* Hanover, N.H.: Published for Brandeis University Press by the University Press of New England, 1976.

Karp, Abraham J. *Haven and Home: A History of the Jews in America.* New York: Schocken Books, 1985.

Neusner, Jacob, ed. *Understanding American Judaism: Toward the Description of a Modern Religion.* Vol. 1: *The Rabbi and the Synagogue.* Vol. 2: *Sectors of American Judaism: Reform, Orthodoxy, Conservatism, and Reconstructionism.* New York: Ktav Publishing House, 1975.

Waxman, Chaim. *America's Jews in Transition.* Philadelphia: Temple University Press, 1983.

CONSERVATIVE JUDAISM

Davis, Moshe. *The Emergence of Conservative Judaism.* Philadelphia: Jewish Publication Society, 1963.

Dorff, Elliot N. *Conservative Judaism: Our Ancestors to Our Descendants.* New York: Youth Commission, United Synagogue of America, 1977.

Rosenblum, Herbert. *Conservative Judaism: A Contemporary History.* New

York: United Synagogue of America, 1983.

Sklare, Marshall. *Conservative Judaism: An American Religious Movement.* New ed. New York: Schocken Books, 1972.

ORTHODOX JUDAISM

Bulka, Reuven P., ed. *Dimensions of Orthodox Judaism.* New York: Ktav Publishing House, 1983.

Liebman, Charles S. "Orthodoxy in American Jewish Life," *American Jewish Year Book.* 66 (1965): 21-97. (See first listing under "Judaism" for bibliographic information.)

RECONSTRUCTIONIST JUDAISM

Alpert, Rebecca T. and Staub, Jacob J. *Exploring Judaism: A Reconstructionist Approach.* New York: The Reconstructionist Press, 1986.

Kaplan. Mordecai M. *Judaism as a Civilization: Toward a Reconstruction of Jewish Life.* New York: Thomas Yoseloff, Publisher, 1957.

REFORM JUDAISM

Fein, Leonard et al. *Reform is a Verb.* New York: Union of American Hebrew Congregations, 1972.

Lenn, Theodore I. *Rabbi and Synagogue in Reform Judaism.* New York: Central Conference of American Rabbis, 1972.

Meyer, Michael. *Response to Modernity: A History of the Reform Movement in Judaism.* New York: Oxford University Press, 1988.

Plaut, W. Gunther, ed. *The Growth of Reform Judaism.* New York: World Union of Progressive Judaism, 1965.

LUTHERAN

Bergendoff, Conrad. *The Church of the Lutheran Reformation: A Historical Survey of Lutheranism.* St. Louis: Concordia Publishing House, 1967.

Bodensieck, Julius, ed. *The Encyclopedia of the Lutheran Church.* 3 vols. Minneapolis: Augsburg Publishing House, 1965.

Nelson, E. Clifford, ed. *The Lutherans in North America.* Philadelphia: Fortress Press, 1975.

MENNONITE

Dyck, C. J. *Introduction to Mennonite History.* Rev. ed. Scottsdale, Penn.: Herald Press, 1981.

Smith, C. Henry. *The Story of the Mennonites.* Rev. ed. Newton, Kan.: Faith and Life Press, 1964.

The Mennonite Encyclopedia. 4 vols. Scottsdale, Penn.: Herald Press, 1955-59.

METHODIST

Bucke, Emory Stevens, ed. *History of American Methodism.* 3 vols. Nashville: Abingdon Press, 1964.

Ferguson, Charles W. *Organizing to Beat the Devil: Methodists and the Making of America.* Garden City, N.Y.: Doubleday, 1971.

Harmon, Nolan B., gen. ed. *The Encyclopedia of World Methodism.* 2 vols. Nashville: United Methodist Publishing House, 1974.

Norwood, Frederick A. *The Story of American Methodism: A History of the United Methodists and Their Relations.* Nashville: Abingdon Press, 1974.

Sweet. William Warren. *Methodism in American History.* Rev. ed. Nashville: Abingdon Press, 1954.

PENTECOSTALIST

Anderson, Robert Mapes. *Vision of the Disinherited: The Making of American Pentecostalism.* New York: Oxford Press, 1979.

Hollenweger, Walter J. *The Pentecostals: the Charismatic Movement in the Churches.* Translated by R.A. Wilson. Minneapolis: Augsburg Publishing House, 1972.

Nichol, John T. *Pentecostalism.* Rev. ed. Plainfield, N.J.: Logos International, 1971.

Synan, Vinson. *The Holiness-Pentecostal Movement in the United States.* Grand Rapids, Mich.: William B. Eerdmans, 1971.

PRESBYTERIAN

Armstrong, Maurice W.; Loetscher, Lefferts A.; and Anderson, Charles A.; eds. *The Presbyterian Enterprise: Sources of American Presbyterian History.* Philadelphia: Westminster Press, 1956.

Loetscher, Lefferts A. *Brief History of Presbyterianism.* With new chapter by George Laird Hunt. 4th ed. Philadelphia: Westminster Press, 1978.

_____. *The Broadening Church: A Study of Theological Issues in the Presbyterian Church Since 1869.* Philadelphia: University of Pennsylvania Press, 1954.

Thompson, Ernest Trice. *Presbyterians in the South.* 3 vols. Richmond:

John Knox Press, 1963-1973.

RELIGIOUS SOCIETY OF FRIENDS (QUAKERS)

Bacon, Margaret Hope. *The Quiet Rebels: The Story of the Quakers in America*. New York: Basic Books, 1969.

Trueblood, David Elton. *The People Called Quakers*. New York: Harper and Row, 1966.

ROMAN CATHOLIC

Dolan, Jay P. *The American Catholic Experience: A History From Colonial Times to the Present*. Garden City, NY: Doubleday, 1985.

Ellis, John Tracy. *American Catholicism*. 2nd ed. Chicago: University of Chicago Press, 1969.

_____. *A Guide to American Catholic History*. 2nd ed. Rev. and enl. Santa Barbara, Cal.: ABC-Clio, 1982.

Hennesey, James J. *American Catholics: A History of the Roman Catholic Community in the United States*. New York: Oxford University Press, 1981.

McAvoy, Thomas T. *A History of the Catholic Church in the United States*. Notre Dame, Ind.: University of Notre Dame Press, 1969.

SALVATION ARMY

McKinley, Edward H. *Marching to Glory: The History of the Salvation Army in the United States of America, 1880-1980*. 1st ed. San Francisco: Harper and Row, 1980.

Moyles, R.G. *The Blood and Fire in Canada: A History of the Salvation Army in the Dominion, 1882-1976*. Toronto: P. Martin Associates, 1977.

SEVENTH-DAY ADVENTIST

Schwarz, Richard W. *Light Bearers to the Remnant: A Denominational History Textbook for Seventh-Day Adventist College Classes*. Mountain View, Cal.: Pacific Press Publishing Assoc., 1979.

Land, Gary, ed. *Adventism in America: A History*. Grand Rapids, Mich.: Eerdmans, 1985.

Neufeld, Don F., ed. *Seventh-Day Adventist Encyclopedia*. Rev. ed. Washington, D.C.: Review and Herald Publishing Association, 1976.

UNITARIAN UNIVERSALIST

Ahlstrom, Sydney E. and Carey, Jonathan S., eds. *An American*

Reformation: A Documentary History of Unitarian Christianity. Middletown, Conn.: Wesleyan University Press; Scranton, Penn.: distributed by Harper and Row, 1985.

Miller, Russell. *The Larger Hope: The First Century of the Universalist Church in America, 1770-1870*. Vol. 1. *The Second Century of the Universalist Church in America, 1870-1970*. Vol. 2. Boston: Unitarian Universalist Association, 1979 and 1986.

Robinson, David. *The Unitarians and the Universalists*. Westport, Conn.: Greenwood Press, 1985.

Wright, Conrad, ed. *A Stream of Light: A Sesquicentennial History of American Unitarianism*. Boston: Unitarian Universalist Association, 1975.

UNITED CHURCH OF CHRIST

Gunnemann, Louis H. *The Shaping of the United Church of Christ: An Essay in the History of American Christianity*. New York: United Church Press, 1977.

Horton, Douglas. *The United Church of Christ: Its Origins, Organizations, and Role in the World Today*. New York: T. Nelson, 1962.

————————————. *Congregationalism: A Study in Church Polity*. London: Independent Press, 1952.

Walker, Williston. *Creeds and Platforms of Congregationalism*. Introduction by Douglas Horton. Boston: Pilgrim Press, 1960.

Zikmund, Barbara Brown, ed. *Hidden Histories in the United Church of Christ*. New York: United Church Press, 1984.

III.   MAJOR INTERPRETIVE THEMES:

THE BLACK CHURCH

Frazier, E. Franklin. *The Negro Church in America* / Lincoln, C. Eric. *The Black Church Since Frazier*. New York: Schocken Books, 1974.

Genovese, Eugene. *Roll, Jordan, Roll: The World the Slaves Made*. New York: Pantheon Books, 1974.

Nelsen, Hart M.; Yokley, Raytha; and Nelsen, Anne; eds. *The Black Church in America*. New York: Basic Books, 1971.

Raboteau, Albert. *Slave Religion: The "Invisible Institution" in the Antebellum South*. New York: Oxford University Press, 1978.

Smith, Dwight LaVern, ed. *Afro-American History: A Bibliography*. Santa Barbara, Cal.: ABC-Clio, 1974.

Washington, Joseph R., Jr. *Black Sects and Cults.* Garden City, N.Y.: Doubleday & Co., 1972.

Williams, Ethel L. and Brown, Clifton L., eds. *The Howard University Bibliography of Afro-American Religious Studies: With Locations in American Libraries.* Wilmington, Del.: Scholarly Resources, 1977.

Wilmore, Gayraud S. and Cone, James H., eds. *Black Theology: A Documentary History.* Maryknoll, N.Y.: Orbis Press, 1979.

FUNDAMENTALISM

Ammerman, Nancy T. *Bible Believers: Fundamentalists in the Modern World.* New Brunswick, N.J.: Rutgers University Press, 1987.

Marsden, George M. *Fundamentalism and American Culture: The Shaping of Twentieth Century Evangelicalism 1870-1925.* New York: Oxford University Press, 1980.

Sandeen, Ernest R. *The Roots of Fundamentalism: British and American Millenarianism, 1800-1930.* Chicago: University of Chicago Press, 1970.

NEW RELIGIONS

Ellwood, Robert S., Jr. *Alternative Altars: Unconventional and Eastern Spirituality in America.* Chicago: The University of Chicago Press, 1979.

Needleman, Jacob and Baker, George, eds. *Understanding the New Religions.* Grand Rapids: Eerdmans, 1986.

RELIGION IN THE SOUTH

Harrell, David E., Jr., ed. *Varieties of Southern Evangelicalism.* Macon, Ga.: Mercer University Press, 1981.

Hill, Samuel S., ed. *Varieties of Southern Religious Experience.* Baton Rouge, Louisiana: Louisiana State University Press, 1988.

_____, ed. *Encyclopedia of Religion in the South.* Macon, Ga.: Mercer University Press, 1984.

Mathews, Donald G. *Religion in the Old South.* Chicago: University of Chicago Press, 1977.

WOMEN AND RELIGION

Bass, Dorothy C. and Boyd, Sandra Hughes. *Women in American Religious History: An Annotated Bibliography and Guide to Sources.* Boston: G.K. Hall, 1986.

Richardson, Marilyn. *Black Women and Religion: A Bibliography.* Boston: G.K. Hall, 1980.

Ruether, Rosemary Radford and Keller, Rosemary Skinner, eds. *Women and Religion in America.* 3 vols. San Francisco: Harper and Row, 1981-86.

Ruether, Rosemary Radford and McLaughlin, Eleanor, eds. *Women of Spirit: Female Leadership in the Jewish and Christian Traditions.* New York: Simon and Schuster, 1979.

Appendix B
Denominational Resources

Explanation of "Resources" Symbols

A   Written guide to the Archives/Collection

B   Clerical records, biographies, papers; records of other congregational officials

D   Denominational records

H   Written histories of local congregations

L   Local church/group records, biographies, papers

P   Published guidelines for gathering information and writing local histories

The following list is a partial one, assembled on the basis of responses to written inquiries. Published directories were consulted for additional verification, but the result is by no means comprehensive.

RELATED ORGANIZATIONS

American Bible Society
Archivist
1865 Broadway
New York, NY 10023
(215) 581-7400

Society of American Archivists
600 South Federal Street
Suite 504
Chicago, IL 60605
(312) 922-0140

Adventist

Jenks Memorial Collection of Adventural
  Materials
Curator
Aurora University
Aurora, IL 60507
(312) 892-6431
Resources: A,D,L

Seventh-Day Adventist Archive and
  Research Center
Curator, Heritage Room
Andrews University
Berrien Springs, MI 49104
(616) 471-7771
Resources: A,C,D,L

Seventh-Day Adventists - General
  Conference
Director, Office of Archives and
  Statistics
6840 Eastern Avenue, N.W.
Washington, DC 20012
(202) 723-0800
Resources: C,D

African Methodist Episcopal

Wilberforce University
Librarian
Rembert-Stokes Learning Center
Archives and Special Collections
Wilberforce, OH 45384
(513) 376-2911
Resources: C,D,L

Assemblies of God

Assemblies of God Theological Seminary
Librarian
Cordas C. Bennett Library
1445 Boonville Avenue
Springfield, MO 65802
(417) 862-2781
Resources: D

Central Bible College
Special Collections Librarian
300 N. Grant
Springfield, MO 65803
(417) 833-2551
Resources: D,L

North Central Bible College
Librarian
T.J. Jones Memorial Library
910 Elliot Avenue, South
Minneapolis, MN 55404
(612) 332-3491
Resources: D

Baptist

American Baptist Historical Society
Director of the Library
1106 South Goodman Street
Rochester, NY 14620
(716) 473-1740
Resources: C,D,L,P

Andover Newton Theological School
Special Collections Librarian
Franklin Trask Library
169 Herrick Road
Newton Centre, MA 02159
(617) 964-1100
Resources: D,L

Baptist General Conference Archives
Archivist
Bethel Theological Seminary
3949 Bethel Drive
St. Paul, MN 55112
(612) 641-6282
Resources: D,H,L

Historical Commission of the Southern
  Baptist Convention
Archivist
Southern Baptist Historical Library and
  Archives
901 Commerce Street
Suite 401
Nashville, TN 37203
(615) 244-0344
Resources: A,C,D,H,L

Primitive Baptist Library
Secretary
Route 2
Elon College, NC 27244
Resources: D,L

Seventh Day Baptist Historical Society
Librarian
3120 Kennedy Road
P.O. Box 1678
Janesville, WI 53547
(608) 752-5055
Resources: C,D,H,L

Brethren in Christ Church

Brethren in Christ Church and Messiah
  College
Archivist
Grantham, PA 17027
(717) 766-2511
Resources: C,D,L

Christian Church (Disciples of Christ)

Disciples of Christ Historical Society
Director
1101 19th Avenue, South
Nashville, TN 37212
(615) 327-1444
Resources: D,L,P

Church of Christ, Scientist

First Church of Christ, Scientist
Archivist
Christian Science Center
Boston, MA 02115
(617) 262-2300
Resources: C,D

Church of God (Anderson, Indiana)

Anderson College
School of Theology
Librarian
Byrd Memorial Library
Anderson, IN 46012
(319) 649-9071
Resources: D

Church of God (Cleveland, Tennessee)

Northwest Bible College
Library
1900 Eighth Avenue, S.W.
Minot, ND 58701
(710) 852-3781
Resources: D

Church of Jesus Christ of the Latter
  Day Saints
and
Reorganized Church of Jesus Christ of
  the Latter Day Saints

Church of Jesus Christ of Latter Day
  Saints
Manager, Public Services
Historical Department
50 East North Temple Street
R240EW
Salt Lake City, UT 84150
Resources: C,D,H,L,P

Reorganized Church of Jesus Christ of
Latter Day Saints
Library and Archives
RLDS Auditorium
Box 1059
Independence, MO 64051
(816) 833-1000
Resources: C,D,L

Church of the Brethren

Brethren Historical Library and Archives
Archivist
1451 Dundee Avenue
Elgin, IL 60120
(312) 742-5100
Resources: A,C,D,H,L,P

Eastern Orthodox

Orthodox Church in America
Archivist
Department of History and Archives
Route 25A, Box 675
Syosset, NY 11791
(516) 922-0550
Resources: C,D,L

Episcopalian

Archives of the Episcopal Church
Archivist
606 Rathervue Place
P.O. Box 2247
Austin, TX 78768
(512) 472-6816
Resources: D,P

General Theological Seminary
St. Mark's Library
Reference Department
175 North Avenue
New York, NY 10011
(212) 243-5150
Resources: C,D

Evangelical

Billy Graham Center
Director of Archives
Wheaton College
Wheaton, IL 60187
(312) 260-5157
Resources: A,C

Liberty University
Dean, Library Services
Box 20000
Lynchburg, VA 24506
(804) 237-5961
Resources: C,H,L

Evangelical Covenant Church

Evangelical Covenant Church of
America
Archivist
Covenant Archives and Historical
Library
5125 N. Spaulding Avenue
Chicago, IL 60625
(312) 583-2700
Resources: C,D,L

Jewish

American Jewish Archives
Director
3101 Clifton Avenue
Cincinnati, OH 45220
(513) 221-1875
Resources: A,C,L,P

American Jewish Historical Society
Librarian
Brandeis University
2 Thorton Road
Waltham, MA 02154
(617) 891-8110
Resources: H,L

YIVO Institute for Jewish Research
Associate Archivist
1048 Fifth Avenue
New York, NY 10028
(212) 535-6700
Resources: L

Lutheran

Concordia Historical Institute
Director
Department of Archives and History
The Lutheran Church-Missouri Synod
801 De Mun Avenue
St. Louis, MO 63105
(314) 721-5934, ext. 320
Resources: A,C,D,H,L,P

The Evangelical Lutheran Church
  in America
Elisabeth Wittman
Chief Archivist
8765 W. Higgins Road
Chicago, IL 60631-4198
(312) 380-2815
Resources: A,C,D,L,P

Finnish-American Historical Archives
Director
Suomi College
Hancock, MI 49930
(906) 482-5300
Resources: A,C,D,L

Norwegian-American Historical
  Association
Archivist
St. Olaf College
Northfield, MN 55057
(507) 663-3221
Resources: A,H,L

Mennonite

Archives of the Mennonite Church
1700 South Main Street
Goshen, IN 46526
(219) 533-3161, ext. 477
Resources: C,D,L,P

Center for Mennonite Brethren Studies
Archivist
Mennonite Brethren Biblical Seminary
4824 East Butler at Chestnut
Fresno, CA 93727
(209) 251-7194
Resources: D,H,L,P

Menno Simons Historical Library
Archivist
Eastern Mennonite College
Harrisonburg, VA 22801
(703) 433-2771
Resources: C,D,L

Mennonite Historical Library
Librarian
Bluffton College
Bluffton, OH 45817
(419) 358-8015
Resources: D,L

Mennonite Library and Archives
Director
Information and Research Center
North Newton, KS 67117
Resources: C,D,H,L,P

Methodist

Commission on Archives and History
Southern New England Conference,
  United Methodist Church
Director of the Library
745 Commonwealth Avenue
Boston, MA 02215
(617) 353-3034
Resources: D,H,L

DePauw University
Archives Coordinator
Greencastle, IN 46135
(317) 658-4800
Resources: A,C,D,H,L,P

Duke University
Assistant Curator
William R. Perkins Library
Manuscript Department
Durham, NC 27706
(919) 684-3372
Resources: A,C,D,L

Emory University
Librarian
Pitts Theological Library
Theology Building
Atlanta, GA 30322
(404) 329-4166
Resources: C,D

Garrett-Evangelical Theological Seminary
Librarian
United Library
2121 Sheridan Road
Evanston, IL 60201
(312) 866-3910
Resources: C,D,H
(Note: Archives of Northern Illinois
  Conference of the United Methodist
  Church)

Marston Memorial Historical Center
Executive Secretary
Free Methodist Church Headquarters
901 College Avenue
Winona Lake, IN 46590
(219) 267-7656
Resources: A,D,H,P

Wesleyan Church Archives and
  Historical Library
Director
P.O. Box 2000
Marion, IN 46952
(317) 674-3301
Resources: C,D,H,L

Moravian

Moravian Archives
Archivist
1228 Main Street
Bethlehem, PA 18018
(215) 866-3255
Resources: D

Pentecostal

Oral Roberts University
Director
Holy Spirit Research Center
7777 S. Lewis
Tulsa, OK 74105
(918) 495-6898
Resources: C,D,L

Presbyterian

Historical Foundation of the Presbyterian
  and Reformed Churches
Archivist
P.O. Box 847
Montreat, NC 28757
(704) 669-7061
Resources: A,C,D,H,L,P

Presbyterian Historical Society
Archivist
426 Lombard Street
Philadelphia, PA 19147
(215) 627-1852
Resources: P

Princeton Theological Seminary
Librarian
Speer Library
P.O. Box 111
Princeton, NJ 08540
(609) 921-8092
Resources: D,H,L

Reformed

Calvin College and Seminary Library
Curator, Heritage Hall
3207 Burton Street, S.E.
Grand Rapids, MI 49506
(616) 957-6297
Resources: A,C,D,L,P

Reformed Church in America
Commission on History
Archivist
21 Seminary Place
New Brunswick, NJ 08901
(201) 246-1779
Resources: C,D,H,L,P

Religious Society of Friends (Quakers)

Friends Historical Library
Associate Director
Swarthmore College
Swarthmore, PA 19081
(215) 447-7496
Resources: A,C,D,L
(Note: Extensive picture/portrait/
illustration holdings)

Quaker Collection
Bibliographer
Haverford College Library
Haverford, PA 19041
(215) 896-1161
Resources: A,C,D,L

Roman Catholic

Catholic University of America
Archivist
Department of Archives and
Manuscripts
Washington, DC 20017
(202) 635-5065
Resources: A,C,D
(Note: Holdings include papers of Abp.
John Carroll and Msgr. John A. Ryan)

Georgetown University Library
Manuscripts Librarian
Special Collections Division
37th and O Streets, N.W.
Washington, DC 20007
(202) 635-3230
Resources: A,C,D,L
(Note: Repository for the Archives of the
Maryland Province of the Society of
Jesus)

Ryan Memorial Library
Archivist
St. Charles Seminary, Overbrook
Philadelphia, PA 19151
(215) 839-3760
Resources: D,H,L

University of Notre Dame Archives
Assistant Archivist
607 Memorial Library
Notre Dame, IN 46556
(219) 239-6447
Resources: A,C,D,H,L

Salvation Army

Salvation Army Archives and Research
Center
Archivist
120 W. 14th Street
New York, NY 10011
(212) 620-4392
Resources: C,D,L,P

Shakers

Western Reserve Historical Society
Director of the Library
10825 East Boulevard
Cleveland, OH 44106
(216) 721-5722
Resources: A,D,L,P
(Note: Holdings include Wallace Hugh
Cathcart Collection of Shaker
Literature and Manuscripts)

Swedenborgian

Academy of the New Church
Archivist
2815 Huntingdon Pike
Bryn Athyn, PA 19009
(215) 947-0203
Resources: C,D,L

Unitarian Universalist

Rhode Island Historical Society
Curator of Manuscripts
Library
121 Hope Street
Providence, RI 02906
(401) 331-0448
Resources: L

Unitarian Universalist Association
Archivist
25 Beacon Street
Boston, MA 02108
(617) 742-2100
Resources: C,D,H,L

United Church of Christ

Chicago Theological Seminary
Librarian
5757 South University Avenue
Chicago, IL 60637
(312) 752-5757
Resources: L

Congregational Library of the American
  Congregational Association
Librarian
14 Beacon Street
Boston, MA 02108
(617) 523-0470
Resources: D,L,P

Evangelical and Reformed Historical
  Society
Librarian
Eden Archives and Library
Eden Theological Seminary
475 East Lockwood Avenue
Webster Groves, MO 63119
(314) 961-3627
Resources: A,C,D,L

Evangelical and Reformed Historical
  Society
Archivist
Lancaster Central Archives and Library
Philip Schaaf Library
Lancaster Theological Seminary
555 West James Street
Lancaster, PA 17603
(717) 393-0654
Resources: A,C,L,P

Hartford Seminary Library
Librarian
47 Sherman Street
Hartford, CT 06105
(203) 232-4451
Resources: A,C

Ohio Historical Society
Head of Reference Services
Archives - Library Division
1985 Velma Avenue
Columbus, OH 43111
(614) 466-1500
Resources: C,D,H

Yale University
Archivist
Divinity School Library
409 Prospect Street
New Haven, CT 06520
(203) 436-8440
Resources: C,L

CANADA

Adventist

Canadian Union College
Library
Box 430
College Heights, Alberta
Canada T0C 0Z0
(403) 782-6461
Resources: D

Anglican

Anglican Church of Canada
Archivist
600 Jarvis Street
Toronto, Ontario
Canada M4Y 2J6
(416) 924-9192
Resources: D,H

Baptist

Atlantic Baptist Historical Collection
Archivist
Vaughan Memorial Library
Acadia University
Wolfville, Nova Scotia
Canada B0P 1X0
(902) 542-2201
Resources: A,C,D,H,L

Canadian Baptist Archives
Librarian
McMaster Divinity College
Hamilton, Ontario
Canada L8S 4K1
(416) 525-9140, ext. 3511
Resources: A,C,D,H,L,P

Christian Church (Disciples of Christ)

Christian Church (Disciples of Christ)
  in Canada
Archivist
Suite 303
55 Cork Street, E.
Guelph, Ontario
Canada N1H 2W7
(519) 823-5190
Resources: D,L

Jewish

Canadian Jewish Congress
Director, National Archives
1590 Avenue Docteur Penfield
Montreal, Quebec
Canada H3G 1C5
(514) 931-7531
Resources: A,C,D,H,L,P

Lutheran

Concordia Lutheran Archives of Western
  Canada
Archivist
Department of Archives and History
The Lutheran Church-Missouri Synod
7128 Ada Boulevard
Edmonton, Alberta
Canada T5B 4E4
(403) 474-5273
Resources: D,H,L

Evangelical Lutheran Church in Canada
Archivist
Provincial Archives of Alberta
12845 102nd Avenue
Edmonton, Alberta
Canada T5N 0M6
(403) 427-1750
Resources: D,L

Wilfrid Laurier University
Archivist
Eastern Synod
Evangelical Lutheran Church in Canada
Waterloo, Ontario
Canada N2L 3C5
(519) 884-1970
Resources: C,D,L

Mennonite

Centre for Mennonite Brethren Studies
  in Canada
Conference Archivist
1-169 Riverton Avenue
Winnipeg, Manitoba
Canada R2L 2E5
(204) 669-6575
Resources: C,D,L,P

Conrad Grebel College Archives
Archivist
Waterloo, Ontario
Canada N2L 3G6
(519) 885-0220
Resources: C,D,L

Pentecostal

Pentecostal Assemblies of Canada
Archivist
10 Overlea Boulevard
Toronto, Ontario
Canada M4H 1A5
(416) 425-1010
Resources: D

Presbyterian

Presbyterian Church in Canada
Archivist
50 St. George Street
Toronto, Ontario
Canada M5S 2E6
(416) 595-1277
Resources: A,C,D,H,L

Roman Catholic

Research Centre in the Religious History
  of Canada
Director
St. Paul University
223 Main Street
Ottawa, Ontario
Canada K1S 1C4
(613) 235-1421
Resources: A,C,D,H,L

Salvation Army

Salvation Army
Headquarters for Canada and Bermuda
20 Albert Street
Box 4021
Station A
Toronto, Ontario
Canada M5W 2B1
(416) 598-2071
Resources: C,D,L

Unitarian Universalist

Canadian Unitarian Council
175 St. Clair Avenue, W.
Toronto, Ontario
Canada M4V 1P7
(416) 921-4506
Resources:

United Church of Canada

United Church Archives
Archivist
Victoria University
73 Queen's Park Crescent, E.
Toronto, Ontario
Canada M5S 1K7
(416) 978-3821
Resources: C,D,H,L

Index